After the
Soviet Union

THE HARRIMAN INSTITUTE of Columbia University was established by Governor and Mrs. W. Averell Harriman in October 1982. It absorbed and built upon Columbia's Russian Institute, which had been founded in 1946, and is thus the oldest center in the United States for the interdisciplinary study of the Soviet Union and, now, of those republics that constituted the former USSR. The Harriman Institute is a graduate teaching institute, dedicated to advanced training and research on the past, present, and future of these states in a broad range of disciplines—from history to political science, economics to law, language and literature to sociology and anthropology. Integral to The Harriman Institute's purpose is also the public dissemination of information, analysis, and opinion produced by Institute faculty, fellows, and students.

THE AMERICAN ASSEMBLY was established by Dwight D. Eisenhower at Columbia University in 1950. Each year it holds at least two nonpartisan meetings that give rise to authoritative books that illuminate issues of United States policy.

An affiliate of Columbia, with offices at Barnard College, the Assembly is a national, educational institution incorporated in the state of New York.

The Assembly seeks to provide information, stimulate discussion, and evoke independent conclusions on matters of vital public interest.

CONTRIBUTORS

TIMOTHY J. COLTON, Harvard University

RICHARD E. ERICSON, Columbia University

ROBERT LEGVOLD, Columbia University

STEPHEN M. MEYER, Massachusetts Institute of Technology

ROMAN SZPORLUK, Harvard University

THE HARRIMAN INSTITUTE
Columbia University

THE AMERICAN ASSEMBLY
Columbia University

After the Soviet Union

From Empire to Nations

TIMOTHY J. COLTON
and
ROBERT LEGVOLD
Editors

W · W · NORTON & COMPANY
New York   London

First Edition

The text of this book is composed in Baskerville.
Composition and manufacturing by the Haddon Craftsmen, Inc.

Library of Congress Cataloging-in-Publication Data
After the Soviet Union : from empire to nations / Timothy J. Colton
and Robert Legvold, editors.
p.   cm.
Includes bibliographical references and index.
1. Former Soviet republics—History.   I. Colton, Timothy J.,
1947– .   II. Legvold, Robert.
DK293.A38   1993
947—dc20   92-24725

ISBN 0-393-03420-8
ISBN 0-393-96359-4 (paperback)

W.W. Norton & Company, Inc. 500 Fifth Avenue, New York, N.Y. 10110
W.W. Norton & Company Ltd., 10 Coptic Street, London WC1A 1PU

1 2 3 4 5 6 7 8 9 0

Contents

After the
Soviet Union

Preface

Wе have done this book to meet a need. One of the most stunning revolutions in all of history has taken place in our day, ending not only in the collapse of the Leninist experiment but in the disintegration of Europe's last great empire. In its wake, fifteen former Soviet republics are left to struggle with the elemental tasks of building nation-states, in some cases, where none ever existed, of turning a failed, but long-lived authoritarianism into democracy, and of creating market based economies on the ruins of a centrally planned one. They, unlike any peoples before, have been left to struggle with all three challenges simultaneously.

In the circumstance, this is a drama that observers, beginning with those who study this region, should be constantly attempting to evaluate and to put into perspective. Such, however, is not what was yet happening eight months after the August 1991 coup d'état that launched the new era. So we assembled five scholars and asked them to make the broad, summary judgments missing to that point. We asked them to help a general audience understand what mattered in the deluge of events occurring in this region. The essays that follow, therefore, are a first effort to size up the tumultuous, historic forces released by the collapse of the Soviet Union.

They deal with the present and the foreseeable future. They are about what happens now, with the old order in shambles and fifteen fragments of the ex-empire struggling to make of themselves states, struggling amidst a deep economic crisis and rising ethnic tension. They are not, in any fashion, an attempt to explain how all of this came to pass—why Gorbachev's *perestroika* ended as it did, why trying to reform the Soviet system killed it, and why not only a seemingly entrenched political and economic order collapsed, but with it, an imperial state that had survived for centuries. Vast, profound questions of this order deserve an answer, and answers will doubtless emerge, but in other books than this one, in books that will wrestle with these questions for decades, perhaps centuries.

When all the struts and buttresses of an economic and political reality give way, as they have in the Soviet Union, pretending to know the precise shape of things to come would no doubt produce its deserved and ignominious reward. None of us in this book believes for a moment that the surprises are over and that, by looking long and hard at the present, one can see the unmistakable outline of the future.

Instead, we offer a series of judgments at a moment in time, judgments on both the major political and economic challenges facing these new states and their major political and economic accomplishments. We have divided the subject into five large pieces: Timothy Colton writes about basic political trends within Russia and the other successor states; Richard Ericson, about their deep economic crisis and what must be done if they are to move toward functioning markets; Roman Szporluk, about the critical issues of nationalism and ethnicity; Stephen Meyer, about the dual collapse of the Soviet military and Soviet defense industry; and Robert Legvold, about foreign policy and the emerging international relations among these states.

The project was jointly sponsored by The Harriman Institute, Columbia University, and the Center for International Affairs, Harvard University, under a grant to The Harriman Institute from the Carnegie Corporation. Early drafts of the chapters were used as background material for the Eighty-first American Assembly (April 23–26, 1992), devoted to the subject of Western policy in Russia and the other successor states. A report of these proceedings has been published under the title *After the Soviet Union: Implications for U.S. Policy*. The American Assembly expresses its appreciation to the following funders who made its project possible:

Rockefeller Family and Associates
Italian Academy for Advanced Studies in America
Xerox Corporation
Creditanstalt Bankverein
William and Mary Greve Foundation

Although not a very big book, in doing it we have accumulated large debts. One set of these is to our colleagues at Columbia and Harvard, Professors Richard Betts, Robert Keohane, and Joseph Nye, who joined the five authors at two day-long working sessions, and did much to sharpen the focus of the volume. Without their help the undertaking would have been far less interesting and productive for those of us who wrote chapters.

A second set of debts is to Dan Sharp, David Mortimer, and their colleagues at The American Assembly. They worked long and hard to bring this book to publication, and, in the process, greatly eased the burdens placed on the two editors. Every set of authors should be so lucky as to have such generous and self-sacrificing backup support.

Third, we want to thank various individuals who facilitated the preparation of the manuscript: Andrea Zwiebel, the administrative coordinator at The Harriman Institute, for her usual efficient administrative support; Eleanor H. Tejirian of The American Assembly, for editorial assistance; Freda Remmers, for swift copy editing under time pressure; and Henning Gutmann at Norton, for making special efforts in the production of this book.

Finally, The Harriman Institute wants to express appreciation to the Carnegie Corporation, its president, David Hamburg, and its program chair, Frederic Mosher. Without their support, not only this book, but much else would not have been possible at the Institute.

May 1, 1992
Timothy J. Colton and Robert Legvold

LATVIA
Riga
ESTONIA
Tallinn
Vilnius
LITHUANIA
St.Petersburg
KALININGRAD
BELARUS
Minsk
TATARSTAN
MOLDOVA
Chisinau
Kiev
Moscow
Kazan
UKRAINE
THE RUSSIAN
BLACK
SEA
GEORGIA
Tbilisi
KAZAKHSTAN
ARMENIA
Yerevan
ARAL
SEA
AZERBAIJAN
Baku
Alma-Ata
CASPIAN
SEA
Ashgabat
Bishkek
Tashkent
TURKMENISTAN
KYRGYZSTAN
UZBEKISTAN
Dushanbe
TAJIKISTAN

EDERATION

Vladivostok

CHINA

MAP BY BARBARA SHELLEY

1

Politics

TIMOTHY J. COLTON

Getting a fix on post-Soviet politics in 1992 is about as easy as judging a symphony by its opening bars. The ear picks out isolated notes and chords; melody and rhythm elude it. Worse, we risk being misled by false echoes of some half-remembered music. Has the upheaval in the USSR and now the ex-USSR been a replay of the French Revolution, or of 1848, or of the Russian Revolution of 1917? Are present company the ghosts of Bonaparte or Garibaldi or Kerensky? These are questions best passed to the historians, to judge when the orchestra has stopped playing. Grabbing prematurely at analogies with the past is a dangerous game that can foster the illusion of more understanding than is actually there.

TIMOTHY J. COLTON has been the Morris and Anna Feldberg Professor of Government and Russian Studies at Harvard University since 1989 and was appointed director of Harvard's Russian Research Center in 1992. He taught at the University of Toronto from 1974 to 1989. He is a member of the National Council for Soviet and East European Research and a coeditor of the journal *Soviet Economy*. His publications include *The Dilemma of Reform in the Soviet Union* and *Soldiers and the Soviet State* (coedited with Thane Gustafson).

This chapter takes off from the plain and tangible fact that the Soviet regime, in the sense of an organic system of governance and allegiance, has disintegrated. It is helpful to differentiate two dimensions on which this is so.

In the first place, the anti-Soviet revolution that culminated in 1991 has shattered the pre-existing *form* of government. The authoritarian grip of the Communist party of the Soviet Union (CPSU) and its creatures has been broken, and the CPSU as such is no more. Jurisdiction over the preponderance of the territory of the former USSR has been seized by governments that can lay some claim to a democratic mantle, although exceptions and caveats have to be made to this generalization.

The second sea change has been in what Samuel Huntington calls the *degree* of government. Divergent as their values may be, a well-grounded dictatorship and a robust democracy are both orderly polities, where "the government governs" and public business flows through "strong, adaptable, coherent political institutions."[1] In the fledgling successors to the Soviet Union, the opposite is true: governments are hard pressed to govern society and for that matter themselves, and politics is distinguished by the weakness and incoherence of institutions. The master question in post-Soviet politics often seems to be less the classic "who governs?" than "does anyone govern here?"

In short, the good news about advances for democracy in the republics has to be qualified by bad and cautionary news about (1) the incompleteness of the democratic breakthrough, and (2) disorderly behavior that jeopardizes recent gains. Without denying the astonishing triumphs that popular rule has scored, it would be wishful thinking to see democracy as having swept the entire field or as being incarnated in stable institutions.

What They Crafted

The end of the old order was not preordained. The human beings at the top of the Soviet system brought it about by making a concerted and ultimately counterproductive attempt to rectify what they felt at the outset to be budding "crisis symptoms" in Soviet society after a generation of lethargy under Leonid Brezh-

nev. Mikhail Gorbachev invoked the therapy despite the likelihood that, in the words of his nemesis, Boris Yeltsin, "the country's natural resources and the people's patience" would have let
him bask in "the well-fed and happy life of the leader of a totalitarian state" without altering more than its cosmetics.[2]

The announced aim of *perestroika* in politics was to graft onto the
trunk of the Communist regime vines and shoots derived from
liberal principles. First the Politburo eased restrictions on artistic
expression, intellectual inquiry, and, a bit later, on private association. Then in 1988, Gorbachev outlined a daring plan to introduce
multicandidate elections and authentic legislatures. To all appearances, he was convinced that the revitalized tree would stay rooted
in the soil of the "socialist option," that tutelage by the CPSU
could be preserved, if in more enlightened form, and that reform
would buttress both the solidarity of the multiethnic Soviet state
and its status as a global superpower.

Whether or not Gorbachev's combination of objectives was in-
herently quixotic is moot. What matters is that a sustainable amal-
gam evaded him and that the result was an all-consuming and
uncontainable crisis of the regime. Like so many authors of liberal-
izing but not fully democratizing reforms, he found himself occu-
pying a dwindling center, not pleasing either conservatives or radicals. Even after arranging to be anointed the first (and, it turned
out, the last) president of the USSR in 1990, he refused to cast
aside his sclerotic party. The result of his temporizing and zigzag-
ging was the tragicomic *putsch* of August 1991 and the collapse of
Soviet power.

The cornerstone of control, the Communist party, had been
severely damaged long before the tanks rumbled into Moscow, so
that Politburo members were complaining in *Pravda* about their
superfluousness. The coup and its aftershocks ended the suspense
about whether the CPSU would linger on. As it crumbled—and
the point of no return was Gorbachev's renunciation of the general secretaryship on August 24, 1991—the party took with it
chunk after chunk of the overall structure.

What happened to *perestroika* has a vital bearing on politics after
it. One image of transitions from authoritarianism stresses mass
action and initiative from below toppling a diehard antireform

regime. It applies poorly to the Soviet Union. Gorbachev was anything but adverse to all reform, and he was not driven out by crowds in public squares as were, for instance, East Germany's Erich Honecker and Rumania's Nicolae Ceausescu. The humiliation of the coup makers and the follow-through assault on their and Gorbachev's power base were carried out mostly at the elite level. Even in Moscow in August, the crowds were modest; 1 or 2 percent of the capital's populace took to the streets, and some of the most dramatically symbolic acts were the work of municipal politicians and employees. In many parts of the USSR, public participation was limited to watching events on television.

De-Sovietization had more in common with a second oft-observed pattern of rejection of authoritarianism: through bargaining initiated from above over the terms of a democratic exit from national crisis. Usually this happens when progressive elements in the regime embark on "consultations with leaders of the opposition, the political parties, and major social groups and institutions."[3] Together they agree, explicitly or tacitly, on agreements about constitutional revisions, the timing of elections, and the sharing of power during the interim.

If the Soviet case resembles the negotiated "crafting of democracy," as such processes have been described, it also differs from the archetype in important ways. Negotiations over resolution of the Soviet crisis were an on-and-off affair, and toward the end they took a twist not covered by theories of democratization. In 1989 the USSR Congress of People's Deputies, a central assembly elected for the first time on a semifree basis, seemed to be an auspicious arena for achieving a national consensus and promulgating a democratic and genuinely federal constitution. But Andre Sakharov and the few farsighted proponents of such a leap were rebuffed by Gorbachev and the parliamentary majority. The congress quickly degenerated into a debating society divorced from power.

Elections in the fifteen republics in 1990 thrust a new cast of players onto the stage. Reflecting a further year of the liberalization and of the radicalization of public opinion, they had a much more disruptive effect than the earlier USSR balloting. They pushed Gorbachev to explore an alliance with Yeltsin, as of May 1990 the chair of the Russian parliament, based on a radical economic reform known as the "500 Days" program. But, in the end, Gorbachev dropped the idea, never again regaining the initiative. He, in effect, allowed the republics, believing destiny and the population to be on their side, to assert themselves. As they did so, the dialogue over the country's future narrowed to one between them and a wilting and defensive center. The failed right-wing coup, triggered by the scheduled signing of a "union treaty," produced declarations of independence from nearly all of the republics and a new round of largely secret republic-to-republic diplomacy. Finally, and when presented with the Minsk pact of December 8, 1991, replacing the USSR with the Commonwealth of Independent States (CIS), Gorbachev vacated the Soviet presidency and consented to lower the hammer and sickle flag for the last time.

In sum, the Soviet Union's end was crafted, not by representatives of the state in concert with a political opposition and private groups, but by public officials alone, working for the most part behind closed doors. The compact reached was one *among governments*, meaning by this time the cooperating republic governments. Nongovernmental players were not welcome at the table and were informed of what had been decided only after the fact. The symbolism of the event followed quickly. In the August days, the focus of attention had been the "White House," the home of Russia's parliament. With victory, Yeltsin's first step was to occupy the headquarters of the CPSU Central Committee, and in December he could barely wait to move into Gorbachev's presidential suite and the lavish banquet halls of the Kremlin.

During the interregnum from August to December, the crucial bargaining was about the fate of the Soviet Union as an imperial structure. The weak Commonwealth of Independent States signified that the empire was truly dead and that henceforth the republics would be nations ruling themselves. But what kind of rule would that be? Would the now indigenous governors of the republics be accountable to the governed and representative of their will? The deal of 1991 did not speak to this question. On its own, it no more predisposed the emancipated successor states to (or against) democracy, let alone stable democracy, than the granting of independence did for the overseas colonies of Britain and France after 1948.

Protodemocracies and Predemocracies

As a regime type, the Soviet Union and its component parts up until Gorbachev's reforms were a nondemocracy, indeed, an *antidemocracy*. One self-appointed political party had hegemony over all personnel, elections were rigged, spontaneous grassroots organization was almost nil—it was the very picture of tyranny.

In the wake of the fall of the dictatorship, the political complexion of the former Soviet Union is very much a mix. The whirlwind unleashed by Gorbachev has had uneven consequences from place to place. No settlement was arrived at across republics or within any single one offering a durable formula for regulating conflict and accommodating diverse social interests.

In taking brief stock of current political conditions in the individual republics, it makes sense to sort them crudely into two bins. Ironically, republics fit into one bin or the other mainly by virtue of choices made in the two years prior to December 1991. The strongest predictor of the first phase of post-Soviet politics is the last phase of Soviet politics.

Seventy-three percent of the population of the former USSR— the citizens of Russia, Ukraine, Armenia, and the three Baltic countries—live for the moment in what I would categorize as *protodemocracies*. They deserve the classification because they have satisfied the prime procedural criterion articulated in the writings of Joseph Schumpeter, and used by most modern theorists to define democracy: the filling of key policy-setting offices through honest, competitive elections in which nearly all of the adult population is entitled to vote. Only slightly less noteworthy than their having cleared Schumpeter's threshhold is the protean character of democracy in the six pace-setting republics. For them the democratic way is unprecedented—in modern times, at any rate—and is breathtakingly immature.

In all six protodemocracies, the parliamentary elections of 1990—still under Soviet auspices and with the Communist party still extant—were passably fair, and anti-Communist groups, usually under the umbrella of a "popular front," had a chance of winning. In Armenia and Lithuania, they did. In Russia, Estonia, and Latvia, insurgent slates captured a plurality of the seats, then managed to take charge of the legislature following the election. The popular front in Ukraine, Rukh, drew unevenly in different regions of the republic and had to be content with approximately one-third of the seats. Yet it was still able to exercise decisive influence over the government as the Communists' morale waned and the population gravitated toward acceptance of independence.

The legislatures elected in 1990 are still in power in the early post-Soviet era. In Russia, Ukraine, and Armenia they share authority with republic presidents popularly elected in open contests in 1991.[4] The presidential elections were won in Russia and Armenia by the persons installed as chair of parliament at democrats' behest in 1990, Boris Yeltsin and Levon Ter-Petrosyan. In Ukraine, the prize went to a parliamentary chair, Leonid Kravchuk, who wooed the anti-CPSU forces without quite joining them. Outpolling the official Rukh nominee, he also lavished praise on Rukh and put out a nearly identical program. Two of the three presidents, Yeltsin and Kravchuk, are ex–Communist party functionaries. All three, and Yeltsin and Kravchuk in particular, have been astute and resourceful political entrepreneurs.[5]

Nine republics inhabited by 27 percent of the people of the ex-Soviet lands—Belarus, Moldova, Azerbaijan, Kazakhstan, the four units of Central Asia, and Georgia—present a somewhat different picture. They are, in fact, *predemocracies*. In terms of social composition and economic profile, these areas are as a rule less modern than the other republics. Politically, they are no longer antidemocracies pure and simple, in that they have gone some distance in the direction of electoral competition. But they are predemocratic rather than protodemocratic because the change has been less thoroughgoing here than in the rapid democratizers and there has been more backsliding.

The nine predemocratic republics also organized parliamentary elections in 1990, and, except for Georgia, the legislatures chosen that year remain intact. In six cases (all but Kyrgyzstan, Moldova, and Georgia), the Communist party *nomenklatura* had little trouble manipulating the nominations process, keeping nascent oppositions to a small minority of the seats, and securing the selection of the CPSU first secretary as presiding officer of the legislature.

Azerbaijan was the only one of these republics where an autonomous popular front put up a serious fight during the election (it won 10 percent of the seats).

In Kyrgyzstan, the Communists in the Supreme Soviet fell out among themselves after a semicontrolled election, installing as parliamentary chair the head of the local Academy of Sciences, Askar Akayev, and not the CPSU boss. In Moldova, the popular front that took one-third of the seats could not keep a former Communist functionary, Mircea Snegur, from getting the parliamentary chair. Most of the front's deputies had defected by late 1991. In Georgia, the last republic to go to the polls (in October 1990), unsanctioned nationalist groups held the Communists to one-quarter of the seats. The campaign was sadly marred by firebombings of party headquarters, the shooting of several leading candidates, and boycotts of the voting by ethnic non-Georgians and by supporters of concurrent elections to a "national congress" that set itself apart from the parliament.

Seven of the nine predemocratic republics—all except Belarus and Turkmenistan—had popular presidential elections in 1991, and these, too, stand in contrast to the protodemocracies.[6] In Kyrgyzstan, Akayev, the most democratically inclined of the Central Asian statesmen, was the sole name on the ballot. Former CPSU secretaries ran unopposed in three republics—Snegur in Moldova, Nursultan Nazarbaev in Kazakhstan, and Ayaz Mutalibov in Azerbaijan—and harvested from 84 percent (Mutalibov) to 98 percent (Snegur and Nazarbaev) of the votes. The ex-Communist leader Islam Karimov of Uzbekistan and Zviad Gamsakhurdia, the nationalist chair of the Georgian parliament, steamrollered opponents who claimed discrimination against them by election organizers and the government owned media. Karimov got 86 percent of the vote against one adversary, Gamsakhurdia the same ratio against six contenders.[7] In Tajikistan, the winner, though with only 57 percent of the vote, was Rakhman Nabiyev, the republic's Communist party first secretary from 1982 until Gorbachev had him purged in 1985; the opposition accused Nabiyev of squeezing them out of the press and falsifying returns.

As concerns form of government, the predemocracies need to move forward a great deal even in the discreet area of electoral practices before their democratic credentials will command acceptance in the international community. As concerns degree of government, they might seem better buffered against disorder than the protodemocracies, since they have retained more of the hierarchical controls and monocratic style of the Communist age. Yet these assets have already proven brittle, and politics has already been gravely destabilized, in three of the nine predemocratic states.

In Tajikistan, Nabiyev's election in November 1991 capped three months of turbulence that saw street rallies force the resignation of three heads of state (one of them Nabiyev) before his resurrection under suspicious circumstances as president.[8] In Georgia, Gamsakhurdia, having displayed a growing recklessness in policy and intolerance for opposition voices, was driven from the presidential palace by his former prime minister and the national guard in January 1992, only eight months into his term. Enemy militias fought artillery duels in the main squares of Tbilisi, and the elected parliament was discharged. Eduard Shevardnadze, the one-time Soviet foreign minister, was named head of a state council by the architects of the coup in March. In Azerbaijan, President Mutalibov, who also had won in a landslide months before, stepped down in March 1992 when a Baku mob denounced his moderate position on Azerbaijan's vicious quarrel with the neighboring republic of Armenia over the Armenian-populated enclave of Nagorno-Karabakh.

The balance of this chapter will dwell mostly on the six protodemocracies, and in particular on the Slavic giants of Russia and Ukraine, because these republics have the lion's share of the population, more directly engage Western interests, and are easier to study. They have done markedly more than the predemocracies to adopt and abide by democratic rules in the electoral and nonelectoral spheres. This task, however, is hardly done with. Nor have the protodemocracies inoculated themselves against disorder. While none has yet been wracked by the bloodshed to which Georgia and Azerbaijan have been subjected, fear of violence and of a downward spiral into ungovernability is a staple of the press in Russia, Ukraine, and elsewhere and is unfailingly volunteered to foreign visitors. To be realistic about it, these are incomplete, unstable, and unconsolidated democracies-in-the-making.

Institutional Dilemmas

Building democratic regimes in the post-Soviet republics comes down to building and tempering democratic institutions. In the predemocracies, the foundation of unbiased competitive elections has yet to be fully laid. In the protodemocracies, the electoral foundation has more or less set, whereas the rest of the house is only roughed in. In pre- and protodemocracies alike, the new institutional masonry and timber that are in place must be finished and solidified.

Four severe institutional dilemmas loom on the post-Soviet agenda. Democracy builders are searching for workable solutions to: (1) the amorphousness of the policy-setting machinery of government; (2) the debility of administrative structures; (3) conflict over the boundaries of governmental units; and (4) the inadequacy of organizational linkages between state and society.

Amorphous Governmental Machinery

The paramount political institutions of the sovereign republics are suffering birthing and growing pains. This is partly owing to design eccentricities. For example, Russia, like the USSR until 1991, has an unwieldy Congress of People's Deputies over and above the standing parliament, Supreme Soviet, that the congress selects from its ranks according to an abstruse voting formula. Duplication of duties has combined with ideological tensions to spur wrangling over turf, prestige, and interpretation of laws and resolutions.[9]

In general, however, the organization chart broadly conforms to foreign democratic models and exhibits but mild variance from one republic to the next. Lawmaking is vested in an elected legislative assembly, unicameral everywhere except Russia, where it is bicameral and is encumbered by the larger congress. A cabinet chaired by a prime minister answers to parliament and supervises the executive departments. As discussed above, nine of the CIS republics (and Georgia until Gamsakhurdia's ouster) also have by now a president chosen directly by the citizenry; the other republics are likely to opt for direct election shortly. The office is visualized in Gaullist terms: the president is protocol head of state, presents cabinet lists for legislative confirmation, has special powers over public safety and foreign relations, and issues decrees of his own on some domestic questions.

What is bedeviling the republics is not so much untidiness in the apportionment of rights on paper as the incongruence between them and real power and responsibility. While cultural and other underlying variables may contribute, a more palpable explanation is the Soviet inheritance of arbitrary and secretive decision making. As reformers recognized in the 1980s, the gap between appearance and reality could be closed only by erecting a "state of law" in which labels coincide with functions and politics is embedded in rules of transparency, precedent, and due process.

The transition to lawful governance is easier said than done, especially when the institution in question is (1) freshly minted and untested, like any one of the republic presidencies, or (2) stained by an inglorious past, like the republic parliaments, which until the end of the 1980s were abject rubber stamps for the Communist party. A further source of strain has been the resort during the recent turmoil to magisterial edicts and threats in order to compel institutional change. Democratic critics used to fault Gorbachev for raining down directives, but once in power in a number of republics, they have behaved no differently. Yeltsin's hamfisted decrees suspending and then outlawing the CPSU and expropriating the USSR ministries, put out in the autumn of 1991 on the flimsiest of legal pretexts, are cases in point. The corollaries of "neo-Bolshevik" tactics, as some liberals dismiss them, are greater contempt for the law, a temptation on all sides to exploit bans and reorganizations to settle political scores, and the tendency for one edict to follow the other (edict No. 2 often being a command to obey edict No. 1).

Attempts to impose rigor on the institutional setup, chiefly by fostering a clearer division of powers, have thus far had a desultory impact. In Russia, the inauguration of a state presidency and Yeltsin's election to it in June 1991 have yet to forge a cohesive executive branch. Yeltsin's influence remains highly personalized, and the formal array of offices remains a poor guide to actual roles. Illustrative of the problem is the conversion of Vice President Alexander Rutskoi, an Afghan war hero elected on the Yeltsin ticket, into an in-house dissident. Rutskoi has lashed out at the government for "economic genocide" and complained that the Cabinet of Ministers, in which he sits, has been perverted into "a bureau for preparing [presidential] decrees."[10] He maintains separate lines of communication to the press corps, elective politicians, and the military. The scene gains poignancy when one recalls that Yeltsin is sixty-one years old, terribly overworked, and has had coronary trouble. Were he to die in office, his estranged lieutenant would be acting president, until a new election was held, and would presumably stump for the position with the advantages of incumbency.

Plans to professionalize legislatures and to focus their attention on lawmaking have also had an uphill battle. In Moscow, a not atypical republic capital in this regard, relations between deputies and executive officers have soured. Some Western economic consultants have found that before proffering advice they have to adjudicate between the two groups. The legislature for its part has become steadily more fractious. A majority of deputies are of the view that the laws and resolutions they draft and approve have no effect. Most lean against standing for reelection, and some of the smartest are courting other employment, raising questions about their fitness to represent their electors.

Again, inversion of expected roles points to the personalization of politics and the greenness of the institutional lumber. Thus the speakership of the Russian parliament, which was supposed to be a politically neutral job once the presidency was spun off from the legislature, has been drawn as deeply into factional maneuvering as when Yeltsin chaired the Supreme Soviet in 1990–91. Speaker Ruslan Khasbulatov, whom Yeltsin backed for the post, has come out as a harsh critic of the cabinet and sponsors a parliamentary panel for "coordination" of economic policy that is said to be scouting out ways "to interfere arbitrarily in the sphere of competence of the administration."[11]

A fascinating possibility is that some order will be injected into institutional processes in the protodemocracies by the branch of government hitherto moribund in Russia and the Soviet Union: the courts. In January 1992 the new Russian Constitutional Court, its justices appointed for life only months before, took the landmark step of pronouncing a decree of President Yeltsin (setting up a fused police and state-security ministry) unconstitutional, for having usurped the legislature's authority over reorganization of government departments. Without accepting the decision as binding, Yeltsin bowed to it. Not long after that, the court took up the presidential decree of November 6, 1991, that liquidated the CPSU on Russian soil. A voiding of that action would be the loudest signal to date that the rule of law will not always be a slogan in the former Soviet Union.

Administrative Incapacity

Democratic evolution in the republics is also predicated on development of efficient networks for executing the politicians' decisions. Pre- and protodemocratic governments fall shy of the administrative capacity of their nondemocratic predecessors—arguably never that high by international benchmarks—mainly because of the messiness of the break with the hypercentralized world of Soviet bureaucracy.

Concerted government control over civil servants deteriorated all over the Soviet Union in the late 1980s, as chains of command and enforcement were violated and familiar political, financial, and ethical levers were thrown out of whack. Living by their wits, bureaucrats worked out new arrangements with alternative protectors and benefactors and began to treat instructions from line superiors as advisory rather than mandatory. The local apparatus of the CPSU, the backstop to governmental authority for decades, first decayed and then, in 1991, was destroyed.

The issue has taken on whole new dimensions with the dismantlement of the central governmental superstructure. The myriad bureaus subordinated to the USSR have gone separate ways. The armed forces and one or two auxiliaries were transferred to the fragile CIS, although most funding comes from Russia; they will in all probability be subdivided among the republics. Some civilian departments, such as the dissolved USSR ministries for health care or higher education, have been parcelled into republic miniatures. Other agencies, mostly those performing economic overhead or foreign policy tasks (the USSR State Bank, for one, or the KGB's espionage wing), have been appropriated by the government of Russia, to understandable protest from the other republics, angry at being cheated of their fair share.

There are special concerns about the elephantine ministries that for decades administered branches of Soviet defense and civilian industry. The rump Gorbachev government began in late 1991 to disaggregate them into product-specific firms miscellaneously entitled corporations, companies, holding companies, and concerns. The republics distrusted this *démarche,* suspecting a ruse for perpetuation of the dominion of the Soviet managerial class. They have now inherited the problem, and have also begun to examine oversight of the thousands of state economic agencies under their and municipal auspices.

For marketizing economic reformers, the way to handle these entities, the repository of most of the ex-Soviet nations' social capital, is to chop them into competing enterprises and to endow employees, shareholders, or some blend of the two with property rights. There are as of this writing no codified procedures for guiding the switchover. There is no confidence, moreover, about the elementary point of who holds the reins of these organizations now. "So far all that is clear is that all sides are arguing" and that "wild privatization," at times little more than embezzlement by staff and superiors, is gathering steam. "Legislation to date provides no mechanism for a civilized way to destatize. Since there is no system, we have here a nutrient medium for abuses in its realization, bribe taking, kickbacks, and improvisation."[12]

The thing to emphasize is that privatization is not merely an economic topic. Rampant uncertainty about who owns what will be as injurious to political institutions as to production statistics. The democratizing republic governments can assert and reassert control over their administrative extensions, and persuade citizens of the upstandingness of governmental operations, only to the extent that the line between public and private activity is drawn.

Territorial Fragmentation

Uncertainty is also rife about the proper boundaries between governments. There is no optimal size for a democratic polity. A democracy is, nonetheless, difficult to build or stabilize under conditions of intense conflict over boundaries. This is precisely what is found in many of the post-Soviet republics.

Perestroika, by sharpening group consciousness and opening the floodgates to mass politics, generated friction (1) between the central state and the republics, and (2) between the republics and explicit and implicit subunits within them, most markedly the twenty ethnically demarcated "autonomous republics" recognized within the union republics by Soviet law. The meltdown of the imperial center has obviated the first phenomenon but done nothing about the second, which continues to fester. As Roman Szporluk explains in chapter 3, this goes on in circumstances of probing debate about how nations, from the 145 million Russians to bands of a few thousand in Siberia, define their identity. Full-blown separatist movements are making the same demands of a number of the republics as the republic leaders were lately making of the Soviet government.

The clashes over boundaries are rarely as straightforward as they might seem. The terminology employed by the spokespersons for intrarepublic ethnic minorities has escalated drastically—from pursuit of "autonomy" and "sovereignty" after the 1990 elections to "independence" in 1991–92—without acquiring precision or consistency. In Russia, the home to sixteen of the twenty autonomous republics and fifteen of the USSR's eighteen "autonomous regions" and "autonomous districts," the definitional issues are compounded by the fact that, alone of the fifteen former union republics, it has nominally been a federation since 1918 (its name was streamlined to the Russian Federation in December 1991).

There is no common understanding of what federalism ought to mean in Russia. Precedent and most public discussion indicate that the prevalent interpretation among Russians is of what in a Western frame of reference would be considered a unitary state with no realizable right of secession and with certain powers delegated to specified areas. The Federation Agreement initialed by all but two regions of Russia on March 31, 1992, is along these lines, but is so loosely worded as to leave ample room for doubt and disagreement. So gross is the demographic disproportion between Russians and non-Russians that it is hard to imagine a standard, two-level federation premised on juridical equality of the partners functioning in Russia, so long, that is, as the lands occupied by ethnic Great Russians remain a social and political unit.

Cultural and political self-determination are, furthermore, not the only pawns in the game. In a series of ethnic homelands, the struggle is as much over influence in the local territory as over relations with the republic center. Conservative politicians from the titular nationality have in more than one case exploited the sovereignty issue to fortify their local power base and cushion themselves from liberal forces on the outside. In Tatarstan in the Russian Federation, for example, the president who sponsored the March 1992 referendum on independence, Mintimer Shaimiyev, is a former first secretary of the regional CPSU committee who sided with the abortive Moscow coup in 1991.

Then there are the economic stakes. Russia's autonomous republics occupy 27 percent of its land surface (18 percent in the Yakutia republic in Siberia alone). A number of them are resource rich, especially Tatarstan and Chechen-Ingushetia (with large petroleum reserves) and Yakutia (with diamond mines as well as gold, natural gas, and oil). Tatarstan, along the Volga 500 miles east of Moscow, and Chechen-Ingushetia, in the North Caucasus, were the two areas not to sign the agreement of March 31, 1992. In Chechen-Ingushetia, religion has also been an irritant. When President Dzhokhar Dudayev swore in a home guard in November 1991 after being elected on a platform of Chechen and Islamic values, President Yeltsin imposed a local state of emergency. Yeltsin retreated after the Russian Supreme Soviet balked at backing him up, but the area's status has not been resolved, and Dudayev has ruled invalid the mandates of representatives from Chechen-Ingushetia to the Russian parliament—one of them Speaker Khasbulatov, a Russified Chechen.

Far from being confined to the Russian Federation, the problem of boundary definition has taken more strident form in several other republics. In the three Transcaucasus states and in Moldova, it has ignited mini–civil wars that have gnawed at the stability of elected governments. President Gamsakhurdia's loss of credibility in Georgia stems in part from his eagerness to cross swords with the Ossetian and Abkhazian minorities. In Azerbaijan, as has been mentioned, Mutalibov's resignation was induced by his perceived inadequacy on Nagorno-Karabakh (officially an autonomous region within Azerbaijan). The fighting in and around Nagorno-Karabakh has cost perhaps 1,500 lives since 1988. In Moldova, combat over the status of the self-declared Trans-Dniester republic, inhabited mostly by Ukrainian and Russian settlers, has within it the seeds of violence worse than that seen in Azerbaijan.

The impression should not be left that centrifugal forces are invariably linked to the national factor. Center-periphery disputes unreinforced by ethnicity have also gained in currency.

Russia, the most sprawling of the republics, is the most affected. A waxing theme in its public discourse has been the drift toward *regionalizatsiya*, the regionalization of government and politics. Local administrators kindled the process in the late 1980s by moving into the vacuum left by the withering of the central planners' authority. The 1990 elections gave them a political incentive to respond to residents' anxieties about the erosion of social guarantees. As in medieval "times of troubles," it has been observed, Russians "are beginning to support whatever power is closest to them."[13]

Rationing schemes to curtail nonlocals' access to community stocks of food and consumer goods are now almost universal in Russia. In the industrial economy, the local authorities have been emboldened by the enfeeblement of vertical supply allocation to substitute their horizontal directives and exhortations, usually without a shred of legal vindication. Lately, regional elites, often in alliance with venturesome firm managers, have warmed to the possibility of sallying into national and international markets with local products (generally minerals or fuels), which they will barter for other goods (inside the ex-USSR) or to reap windfalls in hard currency (in the world economy). Proposals have also been floated for Tennessee Valley Authority–type development agencies in enterprising regions.

Since the crackup of the Soviet Union, some have gone so far as to prepare a brief for an interlude of "feudal fragmentation" for Russia itself. Now that socialism has failed, these analysts claim, Russia must retrace the growth path of successful societies, progressing from feudalism through primitive capitalism toward a thriving welfare state. To achieve this, as much government as possible should be devolved to enlarged regions that comprise natural trading zones, thereby loosening the fetters on self-sustaining production and investment. Drawing on proposals made by regional officials in Siberia and the Pacific zone, pundits have even adumbrated names for the principals in a "confederation of sovereign provincial states": a Far Eastern Region, a Greater Urals Association, a South Russian Republic, a Confederation of Caucasus Muslim Republics, and the like. They have gone on to urge an analogous plan for Ukraine and Kazakhstan.[14] Russian friends have said to me that regionalization might be the one way to turn Russia into a real federation and even, hypothetically, to reknit the remnants of the old USSR.

There is no basis in theory, to repeat, for saying that smaller governmental units would be less hospitable to democratic politics. The problem is not the extent of the boundaries but the conflict that must be endured and managed in order to change them. In the post-Soviet republics, beginning with Russia, it would be wrenching.

Bridges to Society

A stable democratic politics requires broad and sturdy organizational bridges joining the state with the social structure. In the post-Soviet republics, such linkages are inadequate in quantity and quality.

The Gorbachev leadership, to its credit, enabled the laying of far more bridgework than there had been before. It diluted and then to all intents and purposes did away with proscriptions on assembly and association that were as venerable as the Soviet system. This historic concession paved the way for runaway growth of nonstate organizations and for the demise of the dictatorship.

The "informal organizations" that took fire in 1988 and 1989 were initially targeted on ecology and culture and on cheerleading for *perestroika*. It took only months for the most dynamic of them to become highly politicized and to cross over into either vigorous single-issue interest groups or broadly gauged opposition movements. Many of the mass movements were quasi-political parties by 1990 and played an indispensable part in routing Communists at the ballot box. In Russia, the quasi party was Democratic Russia, an alliance of reform Communists and non-CPSU radicals put together in a rush around a fuzzy program of political and economic Westernization; in the non-Russian republics, the rallying cry was generally national rebirth and sovereignty.

Why would the constellation of organizations that helped inter communism not carry the republics smoothly into a new age of orderly political pluralism? Scattered evidence on the issue advocacy groups shows a hefty number of the "Green" environmental and lifestyle associations prominent at the end of the 1980s to have faded from sight. They have been submerged by absorption into nationalist and other wide-bore political groups, co-optation of their leaders into governmental posts, symbolic local victories (such as cancellation of noxious works projects) that have eliminated galvanizing causes, and shifts in public taste.

In contrast to the right-wing dictatorships that have buckled in many regions of the world in the last two decades, Soviet rule was synonymous with suppression of private economic production, extinction of nonstate media of communication and learning, and abolition or subjugation of the social molecules of traditional life, such as religious, agrarian, and cultural bodies. Therefore, political decompression in the Soviet Union was not followed by the immediate and spontaneous efflorescence, as witnessed in a Spain or an Argentina, of organizations dedicated to defense and promotion of temporarily dormant societal interests.

Only now is a first cohort of groups claiming to speak for producer interests filing into the political arena. Business groups active in the Russian Federation in early 1992 included the Russian Union of Industrialists and Entrepreneurs, the Congress of Commodity Exchanges, the Moscow Bankers League, the Association of Joint Enterprises, the League of Cooperatives and Entrepreneurs, the League of Industrialists, the Union of Small Enterprises, the Congress of Russian Business Circles, and the Association of Peasant Households and Agricultural Cooperatives. Many of these are top-down organizations with tenuous connections to their members and prospective members, but they or some like them will find a conspicuous place in post-Soviet politics.

Labor is a socioeconomic constituency of great latent power, as the coal strikes of 1989 and 1991 hinted. The pattern so far is for militancy and political attunedness to differ vastly from industry to industry. Coal miners on the reformist left are matched by neo-Stalinist employee associations on the far right. Most revealing so far, the two poles are outweighed by an inert middle still in the grasp of the established trade unions given monopolies by the old regime. Seeing apolitical adherence to wage demands as their salvation, these organizations are determined "not to take any active position in relation to reform."[15]

As for politicized, general-purpose opposition activity, here, too, there has been tremendous variation, in this instance by geographic area. In the predemocratic republics, the trick for democrats is to push ahead with the construction of even a few pioneering organizations, in conditions where official attitudes range from indifference to icy hostility. In Uzbekistan, the government recognizes only two political parties—the People's Democratic party, which is the Uzbek branch of the Communist party reborn, and Erk, an opposition group with around 5,000 adherents—and one republic-wide political front, Birlik, whose membership has been dropping.

The police closed Birlik's headquarters, a small two-room office, in spring 1991 and the movement has since had to operate out of one room at the Uzbek Writers' Union. Its leaders endure frequent harassment, such as temporary detention and fines. Demonstrations, the main type of protest open to opposition groups, have virtually been banned since 1989, though unofficial rallies have occurred sporadically.[16]

In the protodemocratic republics, where autonomous movements did invade electoral politics, their predicament stems from their very success. Engendered to depose the autocratic regime and, for the non-Russians, to achieve national independence, they tended to lose focus and elan the nearer their charter goals drew to realization. The catholicity of membership and program that made for instant growth and recognition in the infancy of these organizations leaves them prone to internal stress as they mature.

Many of the neophyte organizations were riven as early as 1990 by rows over whether to collaborate with progressives from the old apparatus and whether to reformulate themselves as disciplined, vote-seeking political parties during the transition period. The crushing of the Communist party and the Soviet empire led toward deeper soul searching about objectives and a tendency to splinter. Most of the popular-front movements, including Rukh in Ukraine, Sajudis in Lithuania, and Democratic Russia, remain alive and breathing. But their leaders have little influence either on their mass memberships, which in many cases are in decline, or on their activists in government, who operate freelance and rarely cooperate among themselves. They seem helpless to stop the proliferation of new parties.

Rukh is split down the middle about whether to go the party route. Its founding chair, Ivan Drach, is opposed and maintains that Rukh can be a big tent in which diverse groups and even parties can coexist.[17] Vyacheslav Chornovil, the Lviv regional governor and former Gulag prisoner who was the runner-up to Kravchuk for president and is now a cochair of Rukh, leads a proparty group. Papered over for now, the fissure is likely to widen.

In Russia, there has been relentless attrition within a Democratic Russia coalition rent by personal, philosophical, and regional rivalries. Three large factions split off from it in November 1991 and formed a Coalition of Democratic Forces of Russia that takes a more centrist position on the nationality question. Its moving spirit is Nikolai Travkin, whose Democratic party of Russia, founded in May 1990, is the closest thing Russia has to a modern political party. The tide is with the new parties popping up at all bands in the ideological spectrum. There is no accurate count of how many there are in Russia, to say nothing of their membership and financial bases. It would be fair to state that the bulk of them are closer to social clubs or discussion circles than to fighting organizations. The public by all accounts could not care less about their meanderings. Tapping this mood, an article on the maiden conference of a Russian Workers' party grumbles that it will be

"nothing more than our 1,001st grouplet for sterile political gab-
bing."[18]

Contextual Problems

There is no doubt that certain social contexts are more nurturing of stable democracy than others. The scholarship on political
development would predict that democratic institutions will be
easier to round out and consolidate if, among other things, (1) the
economy is relatively prosperous; (2) social divisions are not too
deep-seated; and (3) the country's external security is reasonably
well assured.

It takes no great ingenuity to demonstrate that in each of these
realms there are profound contextual problems for the predemocracies and protodemocracies of the former Soviet Union.
Economically, the sluggishness that motivated Gorbachev to
launch *perestroika* is paradise compared to the catastrophic inflation
and drop in production and living standards through which his
successors and the republics are living today. The more aggressive
the economic reform, the more precipitate the short-term slump is
apt to be. Forecasts of a 40 to 50 percent sag in production by the
middle 1990s are commonplace among Russian and Western
economists.

Economic decline, marketizing reform, and the organizational
fracturing that accompanies both are certain to have far-reaching
social implications. There is no reform scenario by which unemployment, which has been kept artificially low by overstaffing and
government subsidy of inefficient enterprises and agencies, is not
foreseen to skyrocket. There is talk of 10 to 40 million ex-Soviets
being out of a job a short time hence, and of the *lumpenizatsiya* or
pauperization of the employees of whole branches of industry.
One calculation is that as much as 50 percent of the entire Es-
tonian workforce may be laid off by 1993.

The anticipated social distress does not end with unemployment. Inflation elicited by macroeconomic imbalance and price
liberalization is wiping out families' cash savings. Privatization is
sure to give rise to much steeper differentials in income and
wealth, cutting against the grain of the egalitarianism inculcated

by generations of socialism. Realignments in the occupational and reward structure will produce meteoric reversals in social status and self-esteem, something already seen in anecdotes of prostitutes and butchers who pocket more than nuclear physicists or government ministers. Ethnic unrest is yet another social headache. The discussion above touched on only the question of governmental frontiers, which is prickly enough. Omitted were linguistic policy, citizenship, affirmative action, and a host of other nationality related issues, any one of which would be incendiary at the best of times.

There is no room for complacency on the international front, either. The burial of the Soviet Union has turned what were spats between provinces of a unitary state into conflicts between separate states that have or soon will have the military wherewithal to pursue them with deadly force. The Commonwealth of Independent States, with only intermittent summit meetings to thrash out decisions and no secretariat to prepare or implement them, seems incapable of subduing the bitterest conflicts, like that between Armenia and Azerbaijan, and has denied itself the information channels that theorists have found to be invaluable in inspiring cooperation in international relations. In Russia, the right-wing press raises the question of who "lost" the internal and external empires in the former USSR and Eastern Europe; some hotheads call for treason trials for Gorbachev and Yeltsin.

These thorny economic, social, and external conundrums have not escaped the attention of the politically literate public in Russia and its sister republics. The bursts of euphoria after the defeat of the August coup and the creation of the CIS have yielded to unease, pessimism, and even despair.

Should we share that black mood? Will contextual problems get so desperate that they will overwhelm newborn democratic institutions and propel the country toward neoauthoritarianism?

An answer must begin with candid acknowledgment of how bleak some of the contextual problems are. An ostrich attitude by the republics or the world at large would be the height of irresponsibility. One can readily stencil doomsday scenarios: a vengeful "Weimar Russia" bullying its neighbors and scuttling its own protodemocracy; Yugoslav-type warfare between Russia and

Ukraine over Crimea and the Black Sea Fleet; calamitous plant shutdowns and strikes reducing governments to paralysis; and the like. There is no way events in the Transcaucasus, where one elected president has fled for his life, another has resigned, and two republics are squaring off militarily, can be read as anything but regression away from orderly democracy.

There are, however, markers that point in a less gloomy direction. In the first place, not all contextual indicators are unambiguously negative. It should not be overlooked that the external environment, for all of the menacing trends in it, has been rendered less inimical to democratic politics by the end of the East-West cold war, and thereby the removal of the cardinal justification for internal discipline invoked by the Communist regime over the decades. The discrediting of Marxist socialism and the ascendancy of the democratic ethos in much of the outside world—for the present—should also hearten democrats in the former Soviet Union. And would-be authoritarians in the republics cannot be unaware that outright abandonment of democratic forms will torpedo their chances of securing economic aid and cooperation from international financial institutions controlled by the capitalist democracies.

On another level, not a few of the contextual changes are the analogue in a different framework of the "creative destruction" that Schumpeter maintained interfirm competition automatically conjures up in a market economy. Now that their ideological underpinnings have been discredited, Soviet legacies such as a museum-grade industrial plant, prices unrelated to supply and demand, and a class structure based more on bureaucratic niche than on merit or contribution to wealth generation do not deserve to be preserved. Short-term pain in these areas ought to make possible some long-term gain for almost all, and a great deal of gain for those well-prepared and well-placed to flourish.

The silver lining in some of the clouds looming over the republics would be irrelevant to politics if no one there were able to detect it and act upon it. But the record of the last several years does not suggest this to be true. Time and again, the very worst has not happened in late Soviet and post-Soviet politics. Epochal changes have occurred with fantastically little loss of life. This has been due in no small measure to the ability of elites and publics to rise to the occasion, digest contradictory information, and take prudent action. Until now the Yeltsins and Kravchuks have set the tone more than the Gamsakhurdias or the gunmen shooting it out in Azerbaijan.

Another consideration has to do with the interrelations between political and contextual, especially economic, variables. Those relations are a two-way street: politics is affected by context, but conversely politics can also have a significant effect on context. It might well be true, for example, that Russia's protodemocracy would be hard to sustain if 20 million Russian workers were thrown out of work by marketizing economic reforms. But it is equally convincing to argue that Russia's imperfectly democratized political mechanism would kick in well before economic modernizers had been permitted to push unemployment to untenable levels. Having undertaken price and credit reforms in January 1992, President Yeltsin was showing signs within three months of pulling in his horns and braking the tempo of the reforms. Inadvisable though the concessions may be from a strictly economic standpoint, they may be politically advisable and may be the only way to keep the reformers in place so that they can try another day.

Without downplaying the enormity of the contextual impediments to tranquil continuance of democratization in the republics, it is worth pointing out that in the several dozen countries that have democratized since the mid-1970s there has been almost no wholesale reversion to authoritarian rule. While few if any of the new democracies have had the social and economic liabilities of the former Soviet Union, many have had serious problems, stretching from guerrilla rebellions and terrorism to hyperinflation and foreign indebtedness.

What is more, there is nothing unique about the unhappiness with democracy and the "authoritarian nostalgia" that one now finds in the former Soviet Union. The citizens of most other recently democratized countries have also betrayed disenchantment with their freely chosen governments' inability to remedy policy problems. Too much Western commentary makes it sound as if the Soviet successor states were the only nations to have objective problems or to become frustrated with the slow pace of responding to them. After their democratic transitions in the 1970s, Spaniards, Greeks, and Brazilians voted out ineffective parties and prime ministers and replaced them with others, keeping faith all the while with the democratic procedure that allows them to do so. There is no reason in principle why Ukrainians and Russians cannot do the same.

As Huntington reasons, disappointment with democracy is a normal companion of democratization and, ironically, an aid to democratic stabilization. Elites and publics have to learn for themselves that governments frequently fail to deliver on their promises and that regular procedures for changing them are all the more essential. "Disillusionment and the lowered expectations it produces," Huntington writes, "are the foundation of democratic stability. Democracies become consolidated when people learn that democracy is a solution to the problem of tyranny, but not necessarily to anything else."[19]

Prognosis

Returning to the theme of building and stabilizing democratic institutions, several concluding reflections and speculations about the future are in order.

A first proposition is that it behooves us in gazing ahead to take the dismemberment of the Soviet Union seriously. Much as they will continue to interact in a variety of ways, the republics are no longer shackled to one another and will no longer constrain each other's development as smotheringly as they did until 1991. Owing to differing social and institutional endowments, the republics have entered the post-Soviet era with differing political configurations, which I have dichotomized as either predemocratic or protodemocratic. That scheme may become less adequate as these states evolve from here on in.

Political heterogeneity on the territory of the former USSR can be expected to grow as individual republics map out their separate courses. Russia's progress toward democracy is already much greater than, say, Tajikistan's. Chances are, gaps such as this will widen in the years to come, making our job of analyzing and

reacting to post-Soviet politics all the tougher. Macroregional interactions across the former borders of the USSR will probably
make the differences greater. The Central Asian states, flanked by
Iran, Afghanistan, and China, are in a very different political
neighborhood from the Baltic states, a ferry ride away from Finland or Sweden. The more these clusters of countries have to do
with the countries on their geopolitical block, the more likely they
are to copy some of their traits and stray from their erstwhile
Soviet compatriots.

A related point is the importance of contingency and human
agency. Individuals always count in history, but it could be argued
that in inchoate environments such as the post-Soviet one—with a
large number of highly volatile variables in play—accidents of
character count more than in better structured environments.
Yeltsin's statement about the influence of Gorbachev's spurning of
"the well-fed and happy life of the leader of a totalitarian state"
can be broadened into the observation that the strengths and flaws
of politicians up and down the ladder of authority have had an
immense influence on the course of events since 1985. Yeltsin's
own role is as good an example as Gorbachev's, and the list by no
means ends here. Would politics in protodemocratic Ukraine be as
pacific as it is today if President Kravchuk and other Ukrainian
leaders had been as confrontational toward that republic's ethnic
minorities as the leaders of Georgia and Lithuania have tended to
be? Can anyone doubt that things might have turned out differently in August 1991 if Gamsakhurdia rather than Gorbachev or
Yeltsin had been on the hot spot?

Another kind of contingency has to do with the sequencing of
events. The influence of objective variables in politics varies with
the order in which they play themselves out. In the post-Soviet
situation, causal factors such as the contextual problems discussed
above may have very different effects depending on the circumstances and on the combinations in which they are evoked by
political actors. For example, Roman Szporluk reports in chapter
3 that ethnic Russians in Ukraine have accepted Ukrainian independence, because they believe that they will be materially better
off in a separate Ukrainian state. But what if Ukraine's economic
traumas, due to mismanagement or some other factor, turn out

after independence to be much worse than Russia's? Were a majority of the Russians in Crimea or the Donbass to conclude that they belong with Moscow and their Russian kin, the Russian-Ukrainian game in Ukraine and between the republics would change in a trice. It is hard to say which would be more wounded, the prospects of nonviolent management of Russian-Ukrainian relations (and avoidance of a terrifying version of the war between Serbia and Croatia) or the prospects of democratic moderation within the two countries.

Comparative analysis tells us that democratic institutions take some time to build and cement, even in the most benign of conditions. Huntington maintains that a good yardstick for democratic consolidation is a "two-turnover test." By this criterion, a democracy may be thought of as consolidated if the party or group that wins the initial free election at the time of transition loses a later election and surrenders office to the winners, and if that second group then peacefully hands over power to the victors in a subsequent election.[20] For the former Soviet Union, even if we consider the parliamentary elections of 1990 to have been democratic—a charitable assumption for the predemocratic republics—there are at a minimum two more rounds of elections to go before Huntington's two-turnover test can be met. In other words, the protodemocracies, if everything breaks their way, could not be considered consolidated democracies until the end of the 1990s at the earliest. For the predemocracies, the wait may be far longer.

All of this is to say that we should not expect settled democracies to appear overnight in the ex-Soviet republics, and we should not rest foreign policy on the assumption that this will occur. By world standards, the raw structures of the pre- and protodemocracies have not had anywhere near as long as they need to sort out roles and norms, educate the populace about their meaning, depersonalize key offices through elite circulation, and weather developmental crises—in a word, to institutionalize in the full sense.

There are two principal grounds, apart from wagering on the settling effect of the passage of time, for being mildly optimistic that democratic completion and consolidation will move forward in at least a significant number of the republics, including Russia and Ukraine. The first is that privatizing economic reform, if one grants that it is going to proceed, ought to be a positive force. In a nutshell, radical economic reform stands: (1) to slim government down, cooling popular expectations about the state solving everyone's problems; (2) to resolve some of the uncertainty about control of state administrative units; and (3) to provoke the development of producer interest groups, the most persistent claimants on government resources in the capitalist democracies, and thus fill in some of the current void between state and social grassroots.

A second factor to be brought out is the pivotal importance of elections. In democratic development, elections are not only significant in and of themselves. They also stimulate the building of effective political parties, much as market competition forces the construction of effective firms. The multitude of parties and quasi parties now on the post-Soviet scene sprang forth either during the 1990 election campaigns, when most of them were illegal and ad hoc, or after the 1990 elections, when they had little else to do other than argue amongst themselves. New elections will give them plenty to do. Elections will give presidential figures like Yeltsin and Kravchuk, who have had as little as possible to do with mass movements and parties, incentives to get themselves involved. Unless the republics adopt systems of proportional representation, electoral contestation will also tend to winnow out weak and silly parties and to strengthen the hand of leaders who advocate more orderly arrangements for intraparty governance and coordination of legislative activity than are in place right now. Party linkages between voters and governments can thus be expected to be much better articulated one or two elections hence than they are today.

Do these rays of hope mean that Russia, Ukraine, or any other republic will resemble a civics textbook democracy any time soon? I would not go nearly that far, inasmuch as the governments of even the most liberal of the protodemocracies are and will be subject to fierce pressures to curb some rights and procedures that are associated with democracy in countries that have enjoyed it for generations but that are not, strictly speaking, part and parcel of the Schumpeterian definition of democracy. The irreducible element of democratization is fair and competitive elections. If worst case conditions prod republic governments to abrogate elec-

tions—and we saw something not so far from that in the plebis-
citarian, single-candidate presidential elections in several
predemocracies in 1991—then democratization will have been
abrogated and the republics in question will have opted for the
time being for a species of neoauthoritarianism.

If, however, a democratizing republic sticks with honest elections, we are still likely to observe deviations from democratic
ideals in several interesting respects. From the point of view of
Western values, we will be seeing in the best case a syndrome of
minimalist, executive centered, protodemocratic government.

For one thing, political executives are sure to demand extraordi-
nary powers to deal with economic emergency and interrepublic
diplomacy. Presidents Yeltsin and Kravchuk have already shown
as much interest in rule by decree as President Gorbachev did in
1990–91. Yeltsin at the deputies' congress of April 1992 spoke of
the need for Russia to operate as a "presidential republic" until the
economy recovers and threats to its unity ease. Legislatures are in
principle better suited to a politics of compromise and negotiation,
but will play second fiddle to executives in post-Soviet politics so
long as they are as fractionated and underorganized as they are at
the present time.

A second conjecture is that republic governments will seek to
tighten controls over elected local and regional governments, so as
to dampen secessionism and rationalize economic reform. Yeltsin
began to appoint presidential plenipotentiaries in all Russian regions in the summer of 1991. In addition, the regions are now in
the process of acquiring appointed chief administrators (chosen by
the president from a list presented by the local council) and representatives of both the Russian parliament and the Cabinet of Ministers. Conflict between these prefects and the local governments,
and among the prefects themselves, will be a major fact of life of
Russian politics in the 1990s.

A third pattern that is showing signs of coalescing is with respect
to intermediation of organized interests. Here the Russian government, in particular, has shown a predilection toward a form of
corporatism: the conducting of privileged negotiations about resource shares with established but not necessarily representative
groups. Since December 1991 Yeltsin's chief aide, State Secretary

Gennadii Burbulis, has been orchestrating discussions with state and private economic elites and with the trade unions over how to survive the shock of marketization and how to get the cabinet's reform message across. No questions have been asked about how well the government's partners approximate democratic models of internal organization—just as well, for the business and labor groups at this stage fall vastly short of perfection on that score. The Yeltsin-Burbulis approach is pragmatic and unsentimental. We will probably see more of it as postauthoritarian governments struggle to stabilize their environments and buy time for their policies and themselves.

Notes

[1] Huntington (1968), p. 1. Huntington listed the Soviet dictatorship together with the democratic United States and Britain as a country distinguished by political order. His characterization reflected reality when he wrote, and would have applied to the Soviet Union as late as the mid-1980s, when Gorbachev's reforms began.

[2] Yeltsin (1990), p. 139.

[3] Huntington (1991), p. 139. Huntington calls this the "transformation" pattern of transition, as distinct from "replacement" from below; he further identifies a third, mixed type, which he calls "transplacement." Negotiated transitions are also suggestively discussed in O'Donnell and Schmitter (1986), chapter 4, and Di Palma (1990), chapters 3–4.

[4] Estonia and Latvia have deferred a presidential election until after they have adopted comprehensive new constitutions and also out of fear that it might disrupt the delicate balance among ideological factions and ethnic interests. Lithuania now appears likely to elect a president before approving a new constitution.

[5] There were six presidential candidates in each of these republics. Yeltsin got 60 percent of the votes in Russia, Kravchuk 62 percent in Ukraine, and Ter-Petrosyan 83 percent in Armenia. There was talk of electoral fraud only in Armenia.

[6] The Belarus parliament did pick Stanislav Shushkevich, an academic with some distance from the Communist establishment, as its chair in September 1991. His predecessor was forced out for not opposing the August coup. In Turkmenistan, Sapurmurad Niyazov, the republic's CPSU first secretary from 1985 to 1990, and then chair of the Supreme Soviet, was named president of the republic by the legislature. In February 1992 he proposed a new constitution under which the president would be elected for a five-year term.

[7] The abuses in Uzbekistan are documented in Commission on Security and Cooperation in Europe (1992).

[8] Khakar Makhkamov, the first to go, had replaced Nabiyev as CPSU first secretary of Tajikistan in 1985 and gotten himself selected chair of parliament in 1990. Condemned by students, Muslim clerics, and others for having supported

the Moscow coup in August 1991, he was replaced for a brief time by Kadriddin Aslonov, who was in turn dismissed by the parliament in favor of Nabiyev. Nabiyev stepped down as acting president during the presidential election.

⁹ In Kazakhstan, there is another echo of the Soviet past: one-quarter of the deputies in its Supreme Soviet were appointed by officially approved organizations, as was the case for one-third of USSR deputies from 1989 to 1991.

¹⁰ *Nezavisimaya gazeta,* December 18, 1991, p. 2.

¹¹ *Nezavisimaya gazeta,* January 10, 1992, p. 1.

¹² *Trud,* January 24, 1992, p. 2 (in an article about the Russian textile industry).

¹³ *Rabochaya tribuna,* January 18, 1992, p. 2.

¹⁴ Sergei Kosarenko and Andrei Neshchadin in *Nezavisimaya gazeta,* December 12, 1991, p. 5.

¹⁵ Leonid Gordon in *Nezavisimaya gazeta,* January 10, 1992, p. 2.

¹⁶ Commission on Security and Cooperation in Europe (1992), p. 5.

¹⁷ The most active parties in Ukraine at present are the Ukrainian Republic party, the Democratic party of Ukraine, and the Green party, all of which are affiliated with Rukh.

¹⁸ *Moskovskaya pravda,* February 18, 1992, p. 1.

¹⁹ Huntington (1991), p. 263.

²⁰ Huntington (1991), pp. 266–267.

2

Economics

RICHARD E. ERICSON

The end of 1991 brought an end to the cohesion of the Soviet economic system as well as the end of the Soviet Union itself. The command economy was decapitated and its regional limbs severely cut if not, in all cases, completely severed. Yet on most of the territory of the former Soviet Union the operational economic structures and institutions of the command economy continued to function, struggling to maintain themselves and their operations. At all levels, 1992 brought a struggle for survival and self-sufficiency, for independence from former and new superiors, and for control over former and potential subordinates. New political

RICHARD E. ERICSON is director of The Harriman Institute at Columbia University, where he has been a professor of economics since 1985. He has done research and taught economic theory and the Soviet economy at Harvard University and Northwestern University. His publications include scholarly articles in *Econometrica, Journal of Economic Theory*, and *Journal of Comparative Economics*. His current research involves economic analysis of problems raised by the transition from a command to a market economy in the former Soviet Union, and modeling industry dynamics in a market system.

power centers tried to assert their authority over economic agents, with varying degrees of success, while regions and large, important producers tried to assert new economic powers to control their economic environment. Without the constraining and disciplining influence of a real money and functioning markets, both financial and commodity, this dismemberment of the command economy has led to growing chaos and a dramatic contraction of levels of economic activity.

In this environment the concept of comprehensive systemic reform is near meaningless. The system has disintegrated, leaving a number of poorly coordinated, internally inconsistent republic and even local "subsystems," each approaching its economic problem from a different perspective. This has led to a number of stabilization, "transition," and reform "policies" pursuing vaguely similar objectives with often contradictory means in different regions and republics of the former Soviet Union. The forces driving this disorganized approach to economic change are largely political and national and, at least in the short run, largely inimical to economic performance and welfare. They imply that changes and their consequences are apt to be quite different in different areas, despite the fact that all are starting from a qualitatively quite similar situation—the legacy of over sixty years of "real socialist" integrated development. Thus the prospects of the different regions and countries of the former Soviet Union vary quite widely, depending not only on their intrinsic economic characteristics formed during the Soviet period but also quite critically on policy choices to be made both consciously and by omission during the critical years of 1992–94. Despite the immediate costs, the political disintegration of the "unified economic space" for which Mikhail Gorbachev so long fought could turn into a blessing for large areas of the former Soviet Union, if it forces an appropriate economic policy response.

To understand the prospects of this area, we first look to the economic crisis reflected in the performance of 1991 with particular attention to its roots. Then we turn to a discussion of the major economic trends developing by the beginning of 1992 and their relation to structural reform and systemic change. Next we discuss the prospects for economic recovery and the development of functioning market systems in the different regions. There the focus will be on obstacles to both recovery and reform, and the specific factors fostering successful economic change and growth in the countries of this area. A final section will address the implications for the outside world and U.S. policy.

The Economic Crisis

The year 1991 saw the beginning of a serious breakdown of economic activity across all the territory of the former Soviet Union. Almost every area of economic activity was hit with a steep decline as virtually all control and most intermediation structures disintegrated. Only inertia in behavior and patterns of activity prevented a far more massive decline with subsequent human tragedy. While some new forms of economic activity and inter-mediation flourished, they did so largely by feeding on the carcass of the old system and remained an insignificant part of even the shrunken volume of overall activity. Political conflict, the drive for nation building, and ethnic tensions exacerbated trends already imminent in the collapse of the command economy, accelerating processes of decline already underway.

Those processes were the natural consequence of the inconsis-tencies and fundamental incoherence of economic *perestroika*. De-mocratization and *glasnost* had led to the breakdown of the author-ity and will to command so essential to the functioning of the traditional Soviet economic system.[1] The embodiment of that au-thority and will, and the institutional cement that held the system together, namely the Communist party, was destroyed by the fail-ure of its last ditch effort to maintain some control over changes, the coup of August 19–21, 1991. The subsequent abolition, or sei-zure by republic—especially Russian—authorities, of the institu-tions of central economic management led to the dissipation of authority and practical control to republic (now "independent state"), regional, and local political authorities and, more signifi-cantly, to major producers themselves. Thus there was a radical decentralization of decision-making authority.

That decentralization, however, took place in a near vacuum of real economic institutions. *Perestroika* had been destructive of the

institutions of the command economy, but had done virtually
nothing to create functioning market institutions. Indeed, in Gorbachev's pursuit of the illusion of a "market socialism" subject to
the control of "financial centralism," *perestroika* had blocked the
development of real money, of real property rights, of real markets
and their necessary supporting financial structures, and of a legal
environment supportive and protective of private (nonstate) economic activity and interaction. Thus the decentralization of decision-making powers led only to chaos, growing corruption, and
"beggar-thy-neighbor" policies of restrictions on trade. The natural consequence was a severe contraction in trade hitting the population both directly in consumption and indirectly through the
disruption of further production due to lack of critical inputs.

The breakdown of authority also meant that money, the ruble,
had to become a substitute in order to maintain economic activity.
That is, it had to become a real money—a true, unrestricted command over goods and services both immediately and in the future—able to reflect value and hence to intermediate and regulate
transactions. And that requires, at a minimum, that money be
unitary and available in only limited quantity, and that prices be
free to reflect true economic value in terms of that money. Unfortunately, none of this was true for the ruble. *Perestroika* dictated the
monetization of transactions (that is, contractual buying and selling for profit) without allowing the ruble to become a real money
or prices to reflect real costs or values. Economic agents received
autonomy without property or the economic responsibility and
incentive that are inherent to it, and were forced to operate within
a bizarre structure of prices and economic valuation, in particular
of assets and operations. Thus they were forced to pursue monetary profits, and a host of noneconomic objectives, in the absence
of real money, real property rights, real economic valuations, and
real markets, as well as of the controlling and intermediating structures of the old command economy. It was a prescription for economic disaster, only mitigated by inertia and the failure of former
subordinates to adapt to the new environment.

That disaster began to unfold in 1991, as can be seen in the
reported economic statistics for the year. They reflect the micro-
economic chaos both from decentralization without property,

money, or markets and from political disruption, and the macroeconomic chaos of accelerating inflation resulting from governmental, and in particular central bank, efforts to mitigate the consequences of the former with easy credit and budgetary deficits. The official economic performance figures reported in the economic weekly *Ekonomika i zhizn'* (No. 6, 1992) are given in Table 1. They cover, undoubtedly for the last time, all fifteen former Soviet republics, and reflect the general performance in each of those areas. More detail is given for the eleven former republics that had, by then, agreed to join the Commonwealth of Independent States (CIS).[2] They show some interrepublic differences worth noticing, as they cast light on the differing prospects of each of these new states.

The regional variation in aggregate production and investment activity was greater than in trade or even per capita aggregate consumption. This reflects the relatively weak linkage between production and investment activity and final usable output in the traditional Soviet economy. Production in Belarus, Central Asia,

Table 1

Indicator	1991 Change
Gross National Product (GNP):	− 17.0%
Net Material Product (NMP):	− 15.0%
Industry:	− 7.8%
Agriculture:	− 7.0%
National Income (NI) (used):	− 16.0%
Consumption:	− 13.0%
Investment:	− 25.0%
Consumer Prices:	+ 196.0%
Producer Prices:	+ 240.0%
Cash Emission*:	+ 480.0%
Credit Emission**:	+ 210.0%
Budget Deficit:	over + 500.0%

*issuance of money
**issuance of credit

and Azerbaijan was the most stable, reflecting the relative strength of the old command structures in those regions. Armenia, Moldova, Russia, and Ukraine showed the greatest disruption of regular production and construction activity, reflecting as much political tensions as economic changes. With respect to consumption, however, the strongest performance occurred in the Slavic core (Belarus, Russia, Ukraine) and Uzbekistan. The greatest drops in consumption occurred in Armenia, largely due to war and the Azeri blockade, and Tajikistan.

Overall the former Soviet republic least subject to economic disruption in 1991 was Belarus; there contracts were maintained, production and trade remained at over 97 percent of 1990 levels, and consumption of most products held up better than in the other former republics. This reflected the relatively balanced structure of the economy and stability and continuity in the political situation—less change took place in either the political or economic spheres. Finally, aggregate inflation, as officially measured, was fairly uniform across the CIS, although there were wide variations in prices of food items in different localities, particularly of Russia, as a result of varying local supply conditions. Thus previously privileged centers of food supply (category I and II cities, e.g., Moscow, St. Petersburg, military industry cities in the Urals) suffered the greatest relative deprivation and faced the greatest increases in food prices.[3] Finally, it is worth noting that the drop in economic activity was everywhere greatest in investment and construction, and in the state provision of services, including transportation.

Economic Trends and Reform

The economic disintegration evident in 1991 continued in early 1992, at least initially exacerbated by the incomplete, inconsistent price "reform" in Russia, starting January 2, 1992, and the echo price "reforms" in most of the other states of CIS. This was accompanied by a growing struggle for control over the money supply among the former Soviet republics and between the Russian government and its central bank. As consumers' goods prices rose on average over three, and on many critical items five to ten, times in January 1992, the other CIS states demanded that Russia provide more cash rubles to insure sufficient liquidity for making wage payments, which were also everywhere increased by decree.

Russia's inability to satisfy these demands added to the nationalist pressure to have a separate currency, and spurred the early introduction of quasi monies in the form of coupons necessary for the purchase of consumers' goods, in particular food. Ukraine led in this movement to protect its population from Russians using rubles, Belarus began serious efforts to introduce coupons, and a number of the Central Asian states expressed a desire to do so, although nothing was done in the first half of 1992. In doing so, they threatened to swamp Russian efforts at monetary stabilization, as well as exacerbate shortages, by flooding Russia with rubles no longer usable at home. Russia responded with threats to introduce its own new ruble, wiping out the ruble holdings of the other states of the former Soviet Union.

Thus a major economic trend was the high rate of inflation in early 1992, driven by the continuing monetization of economic activity without control over the supply of money and credit. A major push, on top of already accelerating inflation, came from the massive Russian price increases in January. This was followed by a gradual lifting of limits on energy and basic industrial input prices in the following months, and the slow but steady surrender to demands for wage increases and income support for the non-earning population, including a 45 percent wage increase in state financed industry on March 1. By summer, Russia intended to decontrol all consumer prices except medicine, public transportation, and baby foods, and begin final decontrol of energy prices. A further boost to inflation came with the weakening of fiscal restraint in April, as budgetary subsidies were increased to prevent the shutdown of large enterprises and subsequent rapid rise in unemployment. Thus by mid-year, Russian prices may be expected to more than double again.

Some states, like Ukraine, were able to slow the process through a combination of price controls, restrictions on the use of the ruble, and the introduction of coupons. Kazakhstan and the Central Asian states maintained price controls over a broader range of consumers' goods than Russia, relying on greater state control of local resources and production, but were still pulled along in the general inflation. Similarly Belarus was able to limit the increase of prices on consumers' goods by virtue of the strong local agricultural economy, the diversity of its industrial base, and the greater discipline and inertia of its state producers. All these states were aided in this by the fact that the primary sources of liquidity, of monetary emission, were in Russian hands, and hence beyond their direct control.

In all cases, controlled state prices faced competition from both legal and black free markets, which siphoned off cheap goods for resale or offered similar goods at a competitive or sometimes even lower price. However, prices in early 1992 tended only to rise, as producers and sellers had yet to feel any significant pressure to sell; soft budget constraints, easy credit, and the lack of any interest in monetary earnings beyond wages and salaries prevented real price competition from developing. Hence items that remained unsold at the new high prices tended to be returned to suppliers and warehouses for storage, decay, spoilage, and theft, rather than being offered at a price that would move them. The structure of production did not change noticeably, investment was held in abeyance, and hard decisions on employment and the development of the firm or industry were avoided.

This avoidance by almost all producers in the state and quasi-state sectors of the critical decisions necessary to adjust to an embryonic market environment was made possible by two key factors. The first was the absence of a real money, a legacy of the command economy fostered by existing financial procedures and institutions and in particular the existence of dual financial circuits. The second was the lack of financial discipline by the government and central bank of Russia, which exercised the greatest influence over liquidity within the CIS. Ruble emission continued unabated at a rate constrained only by the technical capacity of the printing presses, and the bank continued to issue vast amounts of credit, albeit at higher interest rates, to prevent any state enterprises or operations from ceasing to function merely from lack of liquidity. Thus there remained at least two price systems for many industrial goods and resources, vast amounts of enterprise funds convertible into cash for wages as long as rubles were physically available, and a state budget falling deeper into a deficit that had to be monetized, i.e., covered by issuing new money, due to a lack of salable financial assets.

In these conditions the ruble could not become a real money, convertibility remained out of the question, and continuing massive inflation was assured. Indeed, the exchange rate of the ruble against the dollar, fluctuating from 70 to 1 to 230 to 1 illustrated the predicament; its brief recovery in late February only reflected a temporary shortage of rubles due to massive price increases and the inability of the printing presses to keep up with the "need" for cash. In other CIS states, limitations on the supply of rubles and the reliance on the Russian bank for interstate liquidity helped to hold down price increases, while providing a stimulus to the formation of alternate forms of liquidity, such as coupons or a national currency. Still, serious inflation occurred in all those states.

The chaotic monetary and price situation significantly aggravated the already near universal rationing of necessities by local and regional authorities, and growing export restrictions on intra-CIS trade by governments, sometimes in violation of recently signed "trade" accords. This local/regional protectionism, both by direct prohibition and indirectly through the introduction of quasi monies, comprised a further major trend in the post-Soviet states. It led directly to the disruption of trade on consumers' goods and to the breakdown of wholesale and producers' goods trade as states and regions retaliated with export restrictions and new licensing requirements.

The ensuing and growing unraveling of traditional trade and contract relations contributed to the third major trend—the ongoing collapse of production. That trend was further aggravated, particularly in Russia and Ukraine, by Yegor Gaidar's stabilization program that cut state investment by 60 percent and state orders to military industry by almost 80 percent. Coupled with the apparent tightening in February of the bank credits that had supported the continuation of traditional activities by inertia, this forced producers to begin a desperate search for alternative activities and markets, as well as for nontraditional channels through which to dispose of their output. It also raised the specter of massive unemployment in sectors that fail to find such markets.

Taking advantage, where possible, of price liberalization, all producers dramatically raised prices and shifted their output assortment to higher priced items, recouping enough rapidly depreciating rubles to make wage payments, and putting off payment to suppliers who then were forced to take increasing bank credits to keep operating. Where necessary and/or possible, firms and regions resorted to barter, frequently violating industrial contracts to ship valued output to farms in exchange for food for workers or to critical suppliers in return for their product. As disruption of contract supply increased and credit grew tighter, production continued to shrink, threatening for the first time the real possibility of massive unemployment.

Indeed, the growing disruption of both production and monetized trade has generated a further significant trend—regional semi-autarky. In areas in Russia, Belarus, Ukraine, and Central Asia where the old power structure, usually revolving around a major enterprise or industry, remained strong, the authorities have continued and indeed enhanced the paternalistic role of the industry as a provider of social services and welfare. The local industrial product is marshaled as a resource to be bartered with other regional leaderships or major industrial operations for necessary supplies both to maintain economic operations and to support the local population. This is facilitated by the collapse of any higher effective control and a further economic trend—quasi privitization of state assets.

Local authorities and top enterprise management, i.e., the local *nomenklatura*, have taken effective control of economic operations either directly, without legal basis, or through manipulating new legal forms such as cooperatives, joint ventures, or stock societies. For example, they typically retain command as shareholders in joint stock societies, giving nonvoting shares to workers, key suppliers, and major users of their products. Indeed, monopoly power is frequently used to force such shares on buyers (or those hoping to be buyers) of the desired output in order to raise capital.[4] Large industrial operations also attempted to control the availability of capital and credit by creating largely or wholly owned "pocket" commercial banks. These operate virtually without regulation, and lend both the enterprise and local region a certain amount of financial autonomy, supporting the semi-autarky of the local economy.

Regional semi-autarky is also fostered by the necessity of survival in the face of growing breakdown of trade. This is the case in a number of smaller former Soviet republics and in large regions of Russia. In particular it is worth noting the largely trans-Baikal "Association of Siberian Cities," which is striving to create a more coherent Siberian/coastal economy that does not depend critically on the rest of Russia or the CIS.[5] Other areas looking to similarly "protect" themselves include the Urals and the military-industrial complex of Udmurtia.

A final trend deserves emphasis for its promise more than its present development. It is the formation and spread of new, market oriented forms of economic activity. It is limited by all the factors that brought *perestroika* to ruin: lack of real money, lack of financial institutions and intermediation, lack of real property rights and their police protection, lack of market based commercial and contract law, local government misunderstanding and obstruction, lack of access to land or a secure place to do business, limitations on labor mobility, hostility of the population, and destructive levels of taxation. Despite the obstacles, which vary tremendously across regions and states, a small but hearty nonstate sector has arisen. By the end of 1991 it was providing some 15 percent of national income and included some 40 million personal farms across the CIS, and almost 80,000 new business operations in Russia alone, including 65,000 partnerships, 8,900 joint-stock societies, 3,600 business associations, concerns and consortia, 1,300 commercial banks, over 110 commodity or stock exchanges, over 100,000 cooperatives, and over 50,000 private farms. In Russia these operations controlled only about 4 percent of capital assets yet produced over 14 percent of the value of output.[6]

This ratio of capital to output is not accidental. The environment in which these businesses must operate is still quite hostile, and there is virtually no protection of assets or guarantees for the future. Hence there is a reticence to invest; these businesses instead operate hand-to-mouth on the basis of appropriated or leased assets of state or quasi-state enterprises and local governments. Thus most (some 80 percent) exist in a parasitic, or at best symbiotic, relationship to state organizations. This is also true of the some 5,000 business ventures involving foreigners, almost 3,000 of which were active in the first quarter of 1992; all seek to make the appropriate connections granting access to inputs and policy makers necessary to survive in the still nonmarket environment of the CIS.

Stumbling Reforms

All of these economic trends are closely related to the ongoing struggle to remake each of these economies. The universally proclaimed goal is a "normal" market economy, yet there seems variation in how that is understood in the different states, and how far each is willing to go in pursuit of that goal. Within the CIS Russia is taking the lead in forcing the pace of change through adoption of an International Monetary Fund (IMF)–type "stabilization" program. It is a necessary program of monetary restraint, budgetary moderation, and relatively rapid privitization; but it is still far from sufficient to bring about the desired changes in the economic system.[7]

Particularly troubling is the lack of attention to the requirements for a real money, and the obfuscation and delay in defining private property rights. Also troubling is the lack of attention to creating a legal framework that fosters and protects private economic interaction, particularly against social claims and state objectives. The development of a market economy is also delayed, if not obstructed, by efforts to maintain production activity and patterns of interaction that developed in the Soviet period. To a large extent these operations embody a massive waste of resources and an ongoing destruction of economic value, despite their short— and perhaps intermediate—run useful role of providing employment to millions. Real reform and marketization will imply the wholesale closing and replacement of these operations and their supporting organizational structures, and the release of the resources, both material and human, that they tie up. Yet that prospect is rife with political dangers and indeed the possibility of massive social unrest—a social explosion—which may explain the failure to make the changes in money, law, and property that might force such an adjustment.

The negative trends in production and trade, the economic crisis, noted above are apt, however, to lead to, if not force, some of the necessary changes; growing disruption has, at least to a point, a positive role to play. To avoid a total breakdown of monetized interaction, reducing all trade and exchange to primitive barter, Russia will be forced to undertake a true monetary reform. That must involve unifying the money by eliminating the arbitrary distinctions (e.g., dual financial circuits) and restrictions on the use of financial resources that have survived the collapse of the command economy, and will probably mean introducing a new ruble. Urgency will be added to the reform when Ukraine introduces a new currency, the Grivna (at this writing scheduled for the summer of 1992), and other states of the current CIS indicate a firm intention to do likewise. The only way that a new ruble can be avoided is in the unlikely event that the necessary changes are made, unifying and giving firm value to the existing ruble, and an agreement on sterilizing their ruble balances can be reached with the states introducing new currencies.

There is also a desperate need to establish a CIS payments clearing mechanism to avoid further dramatic drops in levels of economic activity and standards of living from the breakdown of even necessary intra-CIS trade. A stable ruble managed by a responsible central (Minsk or Moscow) bank would be desirable, but a more ad hoc mechanism using multiple currencies may be the best that can be done in the near future. In any case, some such mechanism must be created as soon as alternate currencies begin to appear in the CIS to avoid a truly disastrous collapse of economic connections between member states. Again increasing economic disintegration may focus attention on the need for such an institution, thus helping to bring it about.[8]

The overall prospects for both early economic recovery and a smooth transition to a qualitatively new economic system based on decentralized market interaction are therefore poor. And indeed, for systemic transition it is probably good that the prospects for an early recovery are poor. There is much that must be destroyed in the physical structure of capital, production, and interaction before market oriented activity becomes viable and self-sustaining in most branches of the economy. A Schumpeterian "whirlwind of creative destruction" is necessary for the development of new market institutions and interactions, allowing the exploitation of property that creates new economic wealth. Thus we must see a continuing unraveling of production and devolution of activity for necessary structural change to take place.

The breakdown of traditional contractual relations, and indeed of interrepublic and interregional trade, and the search for new interactions even at the level of barter are good for the evolution of the system, if bad for current performance and standards of living. Interstate barriers to trade force a redefinition of production activities, supply sources, and product markets, and hence facilitate needed structural change. Of course such barriers can also disrupt economically rational and necessary connections. Mistakes, sometimes massive, will be made in the adjustment, and new irrationalities may be introduced by market and nonmarket barriers to trade and interaction. But these will soon be revealed in a market price system driven by the interaction of self-interested agents fully responsible for their own economic survival. Such agents will rapidly move to correct mistakes and reestablish necessary relations. Thus the negative trends of the economic crisis carry a silver lining, a ray of hope for positive developments in the future. And if they do foster true systemic reform or replacement, then they bear the seeds of a solid recovery from the crisis and new, dynamic growth in the future.

Prospects for Recovery

Eventually there must be an economic recovery—the revival and growth of economic activity—in each of the economies of the CIS; any collapse is bounded below. The relevant questions are when, on what basis, and how strong will that recovery be. Here we face great uncertainty as the span of possibilities is quite large, and depends critically on decisions yet to be taken in circumstances yet to be faced.

An early shallow recovery, reversing the breakdown of 1990–91, restoring old economic ties, and forcing the maintenance of traditional patterns of production, investment, trade, and consumption, with some adjustment for activities lost in now fully independent states and consequently greater reliance on foreign economic

interaction, is perhaps possible for Russia in union with Kazakhstan and Central Asia; they include enough of sufficiently strong
old structures to make their revival technically feasible.[9] That
would, however, leave them facing the same economic predicament as the old Soviet Union did in 1985–87, with the prospect of
more serious disruption and decline still in the future. The smaller
states, indeed any former republic alone except perhaps Russia,
will necessarily be forced to greater adjustment, and thus must find
any recovery farther in the future. There are still, of course, great
differences possible in the timing and nature of the recovery and in
the nature of the resulting economic system.

Most conducive to rapid, sustained recovery and growth would
be the early, intentional establishment of well-functioning market
economies with a liberal intra-CIS trade regime and supportive,
market oriented governments. Yet that faces many serious political
and social, as well as economic, obstacles. In particular, it implies
the sharpest and deepest collapse in economic activity, with all
attendant consequences, as old structures are swept away allowing
market based activities to develop. It is also conceivable, if rather
less likely, that market based recovery could come about more
slowly as a result of "muddling through" with almost accidental
adoption of policies removing the obstacles to marketization discussed below and freeing agents to pursue market driven activities.
This presumes a certain amount of governmental impotence and
loss of control and would drag out and soften the impact and pain
of transition.

Far less desirable from a growth perspective, but perhaps more
likely, is the formation of a set of semi-autarkic regional economies, each centrally administered to maintain the progressive welfare achievements of socialism. Such a quasi-feudal socialism
would undoubtedly involve the economic breakup of Russia into
relatively coherent, manageable regions interacting autonomously
with each other as well as the other former republics of the Soviet
Union. This might limit the decline in living standards, but it
would surely delay the economic reorganization necessary for
strong recovery and render eventual recovery weak and incomplete. Finally, there would seem to be the possibility of a long
stagnation after the economic collapse is halted, with recovery

being only relative to the bottom hit at the depth of the crisis. This is apt to be the consequence of some combination of continued incoherence in economic policy, unresolved political struggle within individual states as well as the CIS, politically motivated protectionism and economic retaliation against neighbors, and spreading national and ethnic disorder and perhaps intra-CIS wars.

Indeed, many other more or less dismal scenarios might be imagined. All are, however, driven economically by the existing structural obstacles to reform that destroyed Gorbachev's *perestroika* and ultimately the Soviet Union. They are obstacles that will have to be overcome for a robust economic recovery, in any political structure, to take place. Undertaking that task will, however, initially deepen the economic crisis and hence sorely test political institutions. It will be most difficult when fundamental social and economic attitudes and institutions must be radically changed as in a thorough marketization. The necessary changes with disintegration of old structures could easily trigger political forces that obstruct them in the name of political order, economic stability, and social welfare. It is thus as much a political as an economic question, requiring firm, but finely honed, policies maintaining the environment necessary to continue the marketizing reform that must underlie a sustained strong recovery.

Obstacles to Marketization

The obstacles are both institutional and physical. First among the former is the lack of well-defined, protected property rights and a supporting legal infrastructure. Greed and the residual urge to maintain control, as well as the ignorance of local and state governments, are blocking the assignment of real property, capital, and mineral rights and their protection through the police power of the state. Of absolutely critical importance is the right of exit—the right to sell for market capitalized value—which underlies the incentive to use assets for the creation and enhancement of wealth, rather than just its exploitation for current income. As important is the lack of a real money and a functioning financial system. Financial intermediation is critical to extended production and investment, yet cannot develop without well-defined property rights and a real money.

Similarly, there is a lack of social support systems, such as unemployment insurance, and a taxation system to maintain them as well as other (police, courts, public administration, etc.) government activities for a decentralized, market oriented society. Creating these institutions requires only legal and political action that could be taken rapidly, even if their full implementation will take time and patience. There is also a problem in that pride seems to demand advanced, complicated institutions, rather than the more desirable simple forms that would allow greater flexibility and learning from experience. For example, Russia is establishing a European value added tax (VAT) system that is far too complex to be managed by new administrative structures in the confused economic environment of the present transition.

The physical obstacles to recovery and marketizing reform are deeper and less tractable in practice, if not principle. Most significant is the physical structure of capital, of plant and equipment in place, and the patterns of trade and production that its use implies. That structure was built over decades in pursuit of implementing a planned vision of patterns of production and growth, innocent of any knowledge of or concern for economic value. It includes massive facilities, employing millions, that only serve to feed the growth of that structure. Trade within that structure was planned to keep it functioning, with no concern for equivalent value in exchange or for covering the true opportunity costs of that production or of the investment that was required to support and expand it. Prices were set arbitrarily to cover "costs" measured in those same prices, thus justifying the predetermined structure of production and interaction.

This led to the present industrial legacy of hypertrophic heavy and military industry, an overwhelming emphasis on the production of (obsolete) means of production, and an economically arbitrary and irrational pattern of regional specialization and interdependence. In any approximation to market-clearing prices, much of this capital structure and most of the patterns of interaction that sustained it are not viable; indeed many are clearly value destroying. Self-interested economic agents with any alternatives would shut them down and sell off the assets, where possible. That indeed is a necessary, if painful, step in any process of successful marketization, and hence a serious obstacle to sustained recovery in a new economic system. It is a step fraught with political danger; rare is the government that could survive imposing such pain. It is, however, a step that may not require conscious policy decisions so painful to governments if the current chaos and disruption of traditional ties become deep enough to do the job of shutting down most that would not be viable in a new economic system. Thus the independence and economic isolation of the former republics may be useful in fostering necessary "creative destruction," if it does not last too long.

Closely associated with this obstacle are two structural legacies causing very different problems. One is the closely related issue of monopolization, fostered in the past to facilitate ease of planning. Sole producers of critical products exercise near Galbraithian "new-industrial-state" control over both suppliers and users, blocking attempts of other producers to enter the industry or users to search for alternate suppliers. This is however a somewhat artificial problem created largely by the absence of a real money and markets; it will be dramatically reduced if those institutional obstacles are removed. The temporary problem of artificial and economically inefficient monopolies can be solved by administrative breakup, by allowing foreign competition, and by economic incentives for other producers to enter sooner rather than later, if the economic understanding and political will exist. Attempts to deal with the problem by regulating prices and output of officially listed monopolies, without creating conditions allowing real competition by new producers in the industry, are backward-looking and disruptive of the changes needed to bring recovery.[10]

More significant is the ecological catastrophe fostered by the socialist command economy. This also implies that many industrial operations will have to be shut down, even if only temporarily for capital overhaul or replacement. It will absorb massive amounts of capital that could otherwise be used for industrial restructuring. It will also disrupt, for an extended period, energy and resource supplies that are basic to all economic activity. Although this will slow recovery, it need not hinder the other institutional changes necessary to provide for a strong, sustained recovery on the basis of a functioning market system. Indeed, shutdowns for ecological reasons could even further reform by forcing their users to search for more economically rational (cost efficient) sources, and their suppliers to find new markets.

A final obstacle to economic recovery that needs to be mentioned is the social factor. Economic attitudes and understanding are still to a great extent mired in the paternalistic socialist ideology that guaranteed economic security and the social direction of all economic activity. While that is changing, there is a legacy of social attitudes that resists marketizing reforms, and fails to value economic experimentation, entrepreneurship, and risk taking. These attitudes are only apt to be strengthened by the pain of a real systemic transition, involving massive unemployment and dislocation, as well as by a significant drop in standard of living for most in society. This obstacle can only be limited to the extent that the dislocation and suffering can be blamed on unavoidable circumstances derived from the old system; and even then, governments in many states of the CIS are apt to fall even in the course of a truly successful transition.

Critical Factors for Recovery

How these obstacles influence recovery prospects depends on many factors, both political and economic, some of which are idiosyncratic to specific countries or regions. We will focus on five of these before turning to a brief discussion of the recovery prospects of the major regions and states. These factors provide a basis for making conditional statements; more specific forecasting seems impossible in the present fluid circumstances. They highlight critical nodes from which developments might proceed in different directions. They thus provide a framework for formulating informed judgments about the future. Without more specific knowledge of leadership and elites' intentions and attitudes, and the micro details of the political and economic situation at that specific time in the future, it is foolhardy to predict the actual timing and success of recovery in any of these areas.

The primary factor deals with the timing and content of *policy decisions* that will be made regarding money, property, economic and contract law, trade prices, and the financial system. We have indicated above a tightly related set of decisions that needs to be taken in order to carry out a transition to a functional market system, the surest route to a strong and steady recovery. Implementing these decisions depends primarily on the understanding, will, and perseverance of the political leadership, although social and physical factors discussed below play a necessary role. The more rapidly these decisions are made, the sooner the ground can be cleared of the institutional and physical rubble of the command economy, allowing sustained growth of perhaps 7 percent to 10 percent per year.[11] If they are not, there is little chance that a market based recovery will soon occur, and we must look to other factors and other institutional frameworks to understand the potential for recovery. For example, a quasi-feudal structure of administered regional economies interacting through managed trade may be a viable framework for some recovery, as might "muddling through" with sufficient Western support. Such an outcome might limit the extent and depth of the initial decline in economic activity, but the recovery would be surely weak and slow.

Another critical factor that must be weighed in evaluating the prospects for recovery is the degree of *social support* for the government and trust in the leadership. Greater social support means more political capital that the leadership can expend in making the hard decisions necessary for the pursuit of systemic reform, and hence a greater likelihood of creating the basis for a sustained robust recovery. Social support is greatest and easiest to sustain in ethnically and socially more homogeneous polities, and where economic conditions for individuals and families are relatively better. Thus nationalism, as a unifying ideology, can help sustain reform in the face of hardship, as can local agricultural self-sufficiency and the availability of basic foods. Where social support is weak, the authorities must tread more carefully in implementing the changes necessary for sustained recovery, and always face the increased possibility that a social explosion may wipe away any progress or policies. Hence a lack of social support makes more likely a reversion to administrative means within regions and states, with the implication of rather slow, limited, and localized recovery.

A third factor to be weighed is the *structure of economic activity* in a state or region. The strength and diversity of local industry, as well as of agriculture, is critical to the speed with which it can adjust to institutional changes, as well as to the standard of living that it can support in the growing economic chaos of the CIS. A narrow industrial base, with a high degree of specialization particularly in capital and investment goods or "high-tech," poses a strong temptation to "manage" the economy in order to avoid the losses of serious restructuring. Regions dominated by military industry, precisely because of its importance and strength in the old system, fall into this category.[12] A more diversified industrial structure, particularly when associated with a diverse set of agricultural activities, provides perhaps the best ground for marketizing reforms. For then much industry can be shut down, and many capital assets reallocated, without a fatal impact on the local or state economy and standard of living of its population. Of course, the importance of this factor depends on the scope of the polity for which decisions are being taken. Within Russia or the CIS as a whole, if they can be held together for purposes of unified economic policy, diversity is assured, and this factor becomes much less important. Within Uzbekistan, Belarus, or Tatarstan as autonomous entities, it becomes critical.

A fourth, and related, factor that needs to be analyzed in each case is the *degree of breakdown of the old patterns* of interaction and structures of control in the present crisis. Where they are relatively maintained, the transition to a new market system will be dragged out and made ultimately more painful. Where they are quickly and thoroughly broken, a large part of the costs of transition will already have been paid, and the way relatively cleared for building new structures and finding new interactions as a basis for rapid recovery. Herein lies much of the hope for the smaller former republics that are breaking away from the CIS, and indeed for any area in which economic activity depended critically on interaction with other former republics. It is not the case that any truly essential interaction need be lost. It is rather the case that all interaction that survives must be based on equivalent market value in exchange, and hence will be compatible with the necessary radical restructuring of economic activity. A quick and thorough break, followed by intensive economic negotiations, is perhaps the best scenario for marketization in each of these states. Of course, such a break and the immediate hardships that it imposes can trigger political forces that oppose the necessary economic changes. Thus political will, social consensus, and national cohesion are vital for this factor to play a positive role in reform and recovery.

Finally, there is the factor of *political cohesion*, particularly for Russia. As just indicated, a political breakup carries some immediate economic advantages for reform. But it also carries some longer term economic costs. By introducing additional noneconomic barriers to market trade, it limits the gains to be had from a transition to a market economic system in each of the parts of the former Soviet Union. This is particularly true if resource holding/rich areas, or areas astride critical communication channels and transportation routes, like Tatarstan, break off and exploit their monopoly position to sustain administered nonmarket economies engaging in managed trade with the rest. That could dramatically raise the costs of transition elsewhere, increasing the likelihood of conflicting semifeudal polities mired in general economic stagnation.

Prospects for Recovery

Keeping these factors in mind we might hazard a guess as to the likely future of the various states of the former Soviet Union. The Baltic states have made the cleanest break with the past and are rapidly clearing away old institutions and individuals, thus preparing the way for a thorough marketization. The break is allowing them to renegotiate terms for critical materials for which they depend on Russia or other CIS states. They are far ahead in privatizing, and are preparing their own real currencies with the advice and support of their Nordic neighbors. While several years of deprivation still lie ahead, their prospects for a solid recovery are quite good. By the turn of the century they should have recovered fully from the collapse of 1990–93 and be normal, if poor, social-democratic polities.

The other small states of the former union face more dismal prospects, even if more for political than economic reasons. With thorough liberal reform, and independence from Rumania, Mol-

dova could also achieve relatively rapid recovery. It is agriculturally strong and has enough industry to provide a base for restructuring and trade, without incurring too great a cost. Without the
Dniester republic it is also ethnically homogeneous. The key question is thus: how far will it go in adopting the necessary institutional changes for successful marketization? I fear that the answer
will be "not far enough," and that civil war and the pull of Rumania will also hold back recovery. The prospect is for less decline
than others, but relative stagnation into the new century.

The states of the Transcaucasus have even bleaker prospects
due to ongoing war and ethnic strife. The Armenian economy is
crumbling under the pressure of war with Azerbaijan, blockade,
and natural disasters; Georgia without strong central leadership
will disintegrate into three quasi-feudal principalities; and Azerbaijan is increasingly focused and consumed by its war with Armenia. Their only hope of significant recovery lies in general
peace and in developing as small open market economies. It is an
area with evident entrepreneurial potential and a viable agricultural base. But its industry is now badly misintegrated and is collapsing. Massive restructuring is required, and only outside finance will be sufficient. Given peace, it will surely be forthcoming
from national diasporas and, for Azerbaijan, from Turkey and the
Muslim world. Then with sufficient marketizing reform, growth
could be substantial, particularly in Azerbaijan, achieving new
levels of development early in the twenty-first century.

The bigger states of the CIS present the more difficult cases, as
the legacy of Soviet socialism is stronger and more will have to be
consciously changed. The state with the easiest task is perhaps
Belarus. It is ethnically homogeneous with strong agriculture and
broad based industry that is low-tech enough to be relatively rapidly restructured. Economic activity is, however, still severely tied
to the Russian economy, and a radical turn in economic reform
policy has yet to occur. The slump has been far less here, so there
is somewhat less pressure for radical change, and that will probably be avoided as long as Stanislav Shushkevich remains in control. However, there is hope for a dramatic radicalization of economic policy when (if?) Zyanon Paznyak, head of the democratic
opposition in parliament, wins the election expected by the end of

1992. Then we could see a serious tackling of the obstacles to
long-term economic recovery, with an immediate impact of a
sharp downturn and up to two-year shakeout of industry, followed
by the kind of sustained recovery growth that a functioning market
economy promises. The details of policy, such as issuing a national
currency, will of course depend on what happens in Russia, with
which Belarus will inevitably be heavily involved. Again full recovery in levels of economic activity and standard of living could
occur early in the next century.

Belarus is big enough that other futures, implying far less of a
recovery, are conceivable. It may, relying on its relative success
and prosperity so far, attempt to maintain an administered economy with managed quasi markets both internally and with other
members of the CIS or any successor. This would be consistent
with ties to an inadequately reformed, relatively stagnant Russia,
perhaps decomposed along quasi-feudal lines, a possibility not to
be excluded for the next decade. Other scenarios involving substantial ties to the south or west would seem to require substantial
marketization, and thus eventually lead to a more normal recovery.

Ukraine is another state with a wide variety of potential futures,
depending on decisions yet to be taken. It now seems fairly certain
to separate its economy from that of Russia with a new money and
national barriers to trade, despite the dismissal of Oleksandr Sav-
chenko, a central banker responsible for introducing the new
money. That is promising inasmuch as it breaks the old administered ties, and forces new market relations to be established. Also
promising is the food situation and the relative agricultural
strength of Ukraine. This provides a buffer against excessive drops
in the standard of living of the population resulting from the restructuring of industry. There is also sufficient diversity of industry
to support that restructuring, although the heavy and military industry in eastern Ukraine must suffer massive shutdowns and
unemployment in any marketization of the economy. Finally, ethnic tensions are not yet serious, and both relatively liberal state
policies and the relatively high standard of living (available food
supply) indicate that they might not pose a serious problem.

Thus the main question is: when will the critical policy decisions addressing the major obstacles to recovery be taken? Will the Grivna be unitary and managed properly? Will real property rights be assigned and protected? Will most military and much heavy industry be shut down and its assets sold for more profitable use? Will taxes be simplified and held low, and will private financial and physical intermediation be encouraged, and so on? There seems a rhetorical commitment to move in these directions, but enough of the old guard remains in power that little deep change is yet occurring. Again, as in Belarus, new elections and a new leadership seem to be needed for the beginning of a strong recovery in the next couple of years. The alternative is very much the same as that for Belarus—an administered, semimarket/semifeudal economy, managed trade with the outside, and a slow, near stagnant recovery, albeit from a higher level due to the limit on industrial collapse.

Kazakhstan and the states of Central Asia comprise another set with rather mixed prospects. Indeed, their near future is intimately tied to that of the Russian Federation, for which they are an important source of industrial inputs. Kazakhstan is the best situated of these to grow rapidly once real market institutions are in place if it avoids ethnic strife, as it has diversified industry and agriculture, albeit suffering the same irrationalities as in the other states. As elsewhere, government economic policy needs to undergo a radicalization, and apparently could quickly revert to a more command-administrative mode. Indeed if marketizing reform does not succeed, Kazakhstan and the other Central Asian states could readily turn to a patriarchal, administered, quasi-feudal economic structure, building on the legacy of the Soviet period. In any case, there will be a dramatic restructuring of agriculture toward a more sustainable structure and greater self-sufficiency, much to the detriment of Russian industry that relied on Central Asian agricultural inputs. This will limit the drop in standard of living and ease the transition to whatever economic system will evolve. Thus the economic crisis is generally less in this region, as are the pressures for real reform. However, the example, influence, and aid of Turkey are pushing toward real marketization. If it takes hold, the prospects for rapid growth in this initially underdeveloped area are quite good. If not, it will remain an underdeveloped adjunct to the

surrounding regions, in particular Russia, whether reform suc-
ceeds there or not.

That brings us to Russia, reflecting all of the structural characteristics and problems of the old union. It is here that the full
import of our earlier discussion is felt. Even more than elsewhere
policy choices are critical, as less is forced by outside decisions. All
the opportunities, and the full brunt of the costs of transition, are
faced by Russia, with wide regional variation. The Urals and Udmurtia are areas that will be hardest hit, given the predominance
of military and obsolete heavy industry there and the lack of viable
agriculture. The north is similarly handicapped by its severe specialization and dependence on the military and on extractive and
processing industries, and by its lack of an agricultural base. However, the south and center are diversified enough to have good
potential for rapid recovery, if only the economic environment is
rectified. And the northwest shows promise as a commercial, financial, and industrial center despite its heavy dependence on
military industry, if sufficiently radical economic changes occur.[13]
Siberia is an area of great opportunity due to its vast resources,
underdeveloped infrastructure, and serious labor shortage. It
promises to gain most from, and return most to, outside investment once a conducive market environment is established. Finally,
the far east (trans-Baikal) is also an underdeveloped region of great
potential for the same reasons, as well as being the door to the
vibrant Asian economies. It is these areas that would seem to gain
most, and most rapidly, from radical marketization.

The government of Boris Yeltsin has begun to take necessary
steps toward a real market economic system, with the abandonment of central economic controls and the spreading price liberalization of early 1992. But the measures hereto are far from sufficient; monetary reform must follow immediately, property must
be assigned unambiguously and offered for sale, and major industrial operations must begin to be shut down. Commercial and
financial codes and a simplified tax system are desperately needed,
along with a clear, unambiguous demonstration of the Russian
state's commitment to protect private transactions and property.
Without this, large-scale, spontaneous, and self-sustaining growth
of nonstate economic activity necessary to counterbalance the col-

lapse of the traditional state sector will not occur, and Russia faces a catastrophic fall and winter, at least in the regions that are not agriculturally endowed. Then a move to at least locally based command economies built around dominant regional industries, the quasi-feudal model, with regional breakup of the Russian Federation, cannot be excluded as a real possibility.

Thus the range of possible futures facing the Russian Federation remains wide open. The best scenario is that the present government survives, with changes, and learns or discovers what needs to be done to bring the currently embryonic market economy to life. The worst might arise if it falls to a reaction, perhaps even led by Yeltsin himself, that attempts to stabilize the political and economic situation by reimposing discipline and command by central Russian authorities. If that effort were to face widespread resistance, resort to massive violence, and still fail, then what remains of economic order would collapse into true general chaos, with widespread localized civil wars, massive deprivation, and even starvation. Less dismal in the short run, but perhaps as bad in the longer term, would be the success of a reversal of reform, after crushing what would undoubtedly be significant resistance. Finally, there is perhaps the most likely prospect of continued "muddling through" with Western support, well-intentioned but economically incoherent marketizing policies, continued if slowing deterioration in economic activity levels and standard of living, and continued disintegration of the federation, perhaps to the end of the century. But it too could lead to catastrophic failure.

The optimistic scenario presents the greatest political challenge to the government, for it imposes the greatest initial contraction and hence the greatest pain of transition up front. It requires monetary reform, strict budgetary discipline, and a rapid, clear, and irrevocable assignment of property rights, if only by default to those exercising them de facto.[14] It means refusing to support failing economic activities, beyond a period for orderly shutdown and disposal (sale!) of assets. It also requires setting politically painful legal precedents in support of private property and wealth against social and governmental claims, and simplifying and limiting taxation even though that will limit the ability of the state to ameliorate hardship. Further, these policies need to be supported with new civil and commercial codes, providing a stable framework for private interaction, as soon as possible. If these things begin to be done, then the strongest possible case can be made for direct Western and IMF support, easing the inevitable pain of the transition. For they not only begin to remove the obstacles to the development of markets, but also provide the legal and institutional basis for the rapid expansion of nonstate, market oriented economic activity.

If the economic pain proves too great and there is a social explosion and perhaps another attempted coup d'état, the government that comes out may attempt to bring order and stabilize the situation by reversing the drive toward marketization. This would involve reimposing state administrative control and discipline on economic agents, reaffirming the primacy of the state and its social mission, and establishing rationing and social guarantees. Private initiative would again have to be restrained to prevent disruption or undermining of the new order, and the state would again have to resume primary responsibility for economic development. The model is well known, and there are still people in place who know how to make it work.

In principle, this could immediately halt the economic decline, and within a couple of years restore economic activity and supply to pre-*perestroika* levels. But serious resistance from those who hate and fear the old system, and from those who have gained new independence, wealth, and status, would have to be overcome, and that would undoubtedly require, at least initially, a significant use of force. Would there be enough people willing to use, or support the use of, such force? How serious would the resistance be? Would it receive outside support, including from other former republics? The fate of this effort to turn back the clock would depend on the uncertain answers to such questions.

If this effort were to succeed, then Russia would, at best, find itself back where the Soviet Union was when Gorbachev embarked on serious reform. If it were to fail, then Russia would undoubtedly face the worst of all possible economic outcomes— general, localized civil war, full economic collapse to near subsistence levels, and outright famine in areas with poor agricultural endowment. That failure might clear the way for the development of primitive market relations, but it surely would lead to a breakup of the federation and also might lead to the creation of regional warlords with quasi-feudal economic relations among them. In any case, the economic collapse could only deepen through the rest of the century, with any recovery pushed far into the future.[15]

A final, "muddling through," scenario is based on assumptions of continuity and inertia; it too could either succeed or fail. It involves drawing out the present economic crisis for five or more years, with both economic pain and needed changes for growth being dampened by significant Western support. Even in the best case the economy would continue to contract, despite the growth of the private and quasi-private sectors, as the wealth destroying structure of capital, production, and trade only slowly changes due to the lack of real property rights and incentives. Money in this situation is apt to become more real as administrative distinctions and restrictions crumble, but also to lose value rapidly as the government inflates the currency to prevent the dislocation that would come with true restructuring. Such a scenario is also apt to involve growing foreign investment, under special state guarantees, and growing "dollarization" of significant transactions. Success would mean that eventually one must expect property rights to firm up, the economy to bottom out, and an appropriate legal and regulatory framework to evolve for new market based growth. That, however, may take a decade or longer, and the resulting growth is apt to be less robust than with more radical changes. If Western support can be maintained so long, it may even bottom out at a higher standard of living than with more rapid reform. The cost to the West of doing so, however, would far exceed Marshall Plan levels as a portion of GNP.

The failure of "muddling through" could lead to results as tragic as those from the failure of an attempted reversion to a command economy. A social and economic breakdown could result if incoherent policies block the further development of property rights, real money, and market interactions in the face of full decentralization of operational control over economic activity. The disappearance of integrating policies and structures could lead to the rise of feuding autarkic principalities pursuing policies destructive of trade and private initiative in the name of protecting

their population. Even in the absence of organized violence, this
environment would destroy economic activity without creating
anything, thus prolonging the crisis into the next century, with any
recovery only possible on the ruins of a total collapse. Any foreign
assistance or investment would, despite any guarantees, disappear
without impact or trace in the deepening economic chaos.

Whatever outcome is realized depends most critically on policies followed and decisions taken in the immediate future. If a
marketizing Russian government survives its April 1992 challenge
in the Congress of People's Deputies, then there is some hope for
optimism. The already initiated price liberalization, Western advice, IMF pressure, and the actions of the other states of CIS are
driving the Russian government toward a monetary reform,
greater fiscal responsibility, more rapid privitization, and perhaps
even a restructuring of large industrial enterprises. If the appropriate measures are taken, and the country can hold together for
another two years of deepening economic contraction, then the
stage will be set for the rapid growth of a market driven industrial
recovery. Assuming that that contraction leaves Russia at about
half the levels of real output that it had in, say, 1987–88, it could
completely recover that level of output by 2002, although with a
far different and far more desirable structure, thus giving noticeably higher welfare to its citizens.[16]

On the other hand, it may be too optimistic to assume that the
federation will hold together peacefully, even in the more optimistic scenarios. There are four regional/national issues, three of
which could pose a serious threat to recovery. The least important
of these is the potential for ethnic war in the north Caucasus, or
economic sabotage in some of the northern ASSRs. Both of these
will, if they occur, be costly and distracting, but still only marginal
to the prospects for economic recovery. Far more serious is the
drive for independence by Tatarstan/Bashkorstan, which if
achieved would essentially cut Russia in half. This could place a
rent-extracting principality astride all energy, power, communications, and transportation lines from European Russia to Siberia. It
seems to me that only in the case of a general breakup and feudalization of the economy of Russia would this be tolerated. But if
prevented by force, the disruption could set back both reform and
recovery by several years.

Similarly, there is the somewhat more remote possibility of Buryat independence cutting off eastern Siberia at Lake Baikal. A military solution would be costly, but less disruptive than with Tatarstan. Finally, there is the issue of far eastern economic independence. The region has already begun acting without, and sometimes against, guidance from Moscow, and has already created a quasi-governmental organ in the Association of Siberian Cities with its official press, *Siberskaia gazeta*. Here, however, the leadership is more reformist and market oriented than in Moscow, and is thus most apt to pull away if the central Russian reform fails and the west sinks into stagnation and/or chaos. Then the lure of economic integration into the Sea of Japan basin may become overwhelming, and central Russia may be in no position to prevent its acting. Again all depends on policies and outcomes, both political and economic, over the next few years.

Finally, there is the question of the role of the CIS, or its possible successors, in the future of this region. It seems that to have a future the CIS must become only the loosest of confederations. It has some economic logic in uniting an area with a common Soviet legacy of comparative advantage vis-à-vis the rest of the world, but one that will diminish in importance as real changes take hold. It also can fulfill some basic economic functions that all will find in their interests, once national passions and memories subside.[17] These include maintaining a payments clearing (exchange rate) mechanism, maintaining a customs union, providing a forum for trade negotiations, and providing for postal, communications, transportation, electric power, scientific, and other coordination. Indeed dealing cooperatively with the legacy of environmental and infrastructure problems left by the union will be an important function of some interstate organization, even if CIS collapses. Thus we should expect some confederative structure to survive, although it may, in some circumstances, come to consist of semiautarkic regional governments rather than the current states of CIS.

Implications for the Outside

The implications of the preceding speculation and analysis are fairly obvious. Successful reform, creating a liberal market economy in each of these states, is in everyone's interests. However, the costs, both material and human, will be great, and will be borne almost exclusively by the people of those states, threatening to unleash forces blocking such a reform. The alternative is tragic— economic chaos, stagnation, and growing deprivation on a vast portion of the earth's surface, with serious negative implications for the political stability of that and surrounding regions. Ultimately, the human and material costs of failure to achieve a strong, market based recovery may be even greater, and are apt to be spread beyond the old Soviet borders. Thus it behooves the rest of the world to do what it can to aid such a transition and recovery.

That raises the question of how we might influence it, or indeed whether we can influence it at all. The primary thing that the West can offer is knowledge and know-how about market institutions and business operations in a market environment—ignorance in those areas at all levels is a major obstacle to instituting necessary policies and to those policies stimulating appropriate behavioral responses for recovery. Until there is an understanding of what needs to be done and how to do it, there is little hope that the critical configuration of policies paving the way for early, market based recovery will be generated. That knowledge is now slowly developing, but probably too slowly. Thus perhaps the most valuable aid that could be given is massive on-the-ground and selfless advising from a corps of retired business and government executives and/or business oriented "peace corps"; they could most quickly and credibly impart the knowledge and habits needed to build market institutions and make markets work properly. The costs of even a substantial effort in this area would be relatively low, and the potential returns enormous.

Aside from giving advice and encouragement, there is very little that can be done from the outside until appropriate policies are adopted, and major institutional and legal changes are made internally. An IMF stabilization program requires a real money to stabilize. And even a confidence-building fund in escrow is little more than a temporary stop if internal changes making it usable are not forthcoming.[18] Disaster aid to prevent human tragedy is of course always desirable and useful; however, it must not become so large as to undercut necessary internal changes and efforts.

Beyond economic and business know-how, the real need from the outside is for real capital—economically motivated and justified investment in infrastructure and all branches of industry and agriculture. But to be both forthcoming and fruitfully used, this investment requires a sufficiently stable legal and taxation environment, with clear definition and protection of property rights and a real money, so that risks and returns may be evaluated, even if only approximately. Achieving that is going most of the way to a full marketizing reform, so that foreign capital will act at best as an accelerator and not a prime mover of the recovery. Similarly, an international currency stabilization fund can accelerate the process, once a real monetary reform has taken place. There will then be fabulous real economic opportunities, and businesses throughout the world will naturally rush to exploit them.

Beyond the question of the success or failure of reform, the breakup of the Soviet economy carries implications for the neighboring regions. The Baltic states are already moving to join, and are being accepted into, the Nordic economy. Belarus and Ukraine have a natural sphere of interaction in Eastern Europe, particularly if the European Economic Community (EEC) is slow in opening its doors to its East European neighbors. Successful marketization of these states could make the entire region a valuable partner to the EEC in the economic competition with North America and Japan, or a lost opportunity if either of the latter respond more positively than Europe. A marketized and rapidly growing Azerbaijan and Central Asia could become a key part of a pan-Turkic revival led by Turkey, while a more feudal, less economically successful region is apt to feel the pull of Islamic fundamentalism, fueling anti-Western sentiment throughout the South Asian region. Tajikistan has some natural economic affinities for western China, which may fuel potential separatism within China itself, with unpredictable consequences. Finally, the Russian far east, and indeed all of trans-Baikal, feels a strong economic pull to the prosperity of the Sea of Japan basin. That provides an incentive both to rapidly, radically reform and restructure, and to escape the constraints of Moscow. If the incentive is acted upon, particularly if recovery is going poorly in Russia, it may provoke a violent Russian reaction, again with unpredictable consequences.

That all leaves Russia hanging in the center, perhaps with Kazakhstan, too big to be ignored, but probably not easily complementary with any regional economic arrangement. Indeed, Russia's size and resources, both human and material, make it a potentially viable economic region on its own, interacting with all others. If it is a rapidly growing land of economic opportunity, then lack of integration into a larger economic region should pose no problem; all major economies will want part of the action, and the ensuing interaction should foster both greater Russian and international economic success. If, on the other hand, it disintegrates into a stagnant, quarrelsome economic morass, it could pose a severe threat to the stability of all surrounding regions, and hence to international economic development. It is the latter that Western policy must seek to avert through deep interaction, not thoughtless money, even if the former proves to be an impossible dream.

Notes

[1] For an introduction to the nature and functioning of the traditional Soviet economic system see Ericson (1991), pp. 1–18.

[2] The eleven states of CIS are: Azerbaijan, Armenia, Belarus, Kazakhstan, Kyrgyzstan, Moldova, Russia, Tajikistan, Turkmenistan, Uzbekistan, and Ukraine.

[3] These were also the cities targeted for most emergency aid by the Group of Seven. These trends were closely tracked in the Moscow economic weekly *Kommersant* throughout 1991.

[4] A classic example is "KamAz" in Naberezhnye Chelny, Tatarstan, the monopoly producer of large long-haul trucks.

[5] The ideas and dreams of this group are regularly laid out in their official organ, *Siberskaia gazeta,* published in Novosibirsk.

[6] *Ekonomika i zhizn',* No. 4, 1992. Many are just fictions for the takeover of state operations by management, and are largely vehicles for rent seeking and asset stripping by that management.

[7] At present, the full program has not been published—indeed it may still be evolving. What we know of it comes from speeches of Boris Yeltsin, Yegor Gaidar, and other government leaders, and statements of reported advisors, as reported in the press. What is NOT said seems as important as what is.

[8] Even Ukraine has indicated some desire for this level of economic integration, if the clearing system is independent of, and not dominated by, Russia.

[9] The feasibility of this reversal depends on the willingness of a sufficient number of managers and enforcers to participate. If those in key operational positions resist, then violence may be necessary, raising larger political questions.

[10] This unfortunately was the policy of the Yeltsin government in February 1992, reflected in decrees published in *Ekonomika i zhizn',* Nos. 5 and 6, 1992.

[11] This is the range of rates of growth sustained for at least a decade in Germany and Japan on recovering from the war, in the Asian newly industrializing countries following economic liberalization, and in virtually all Western market economies during their take-off stage of development. It thus seems eminently reasonable for institutionally restructured and recovering market economies of the CIS, at least individually if other member states have failed to undertake similar necessary reforms.

[12] Military industry is a particular problem only because it is so impervious to cost considerations. Were it able to produce and *sell for a profit* at real market prices of all inputs (land, capital, labor, resources, energy, materials, components, etc.) as well as its output, then military industry could become a valuable asset to a free trading region. Slovakia is, probably in vain, putting its hopes on this.

[13] Military industry might provide a base for export led recovery and growth if it were able to become cost efficient and market oriented in a way that no other military industry has ever done before. The likelihood of this is extremely low, despite the hopes of those involved.

[14] So called wild privitization by formerly privileged individuals (the *nomenklatura*) with present de facto control will undoubtedly play a major role in any rapid assignment of property rights, as required for real market oriented behavior. While morally questionable and politically explosive, it may be economically necessary to prevent the serious distortion and/or breakdown of new market mechanisms.

[15] Of course, nothing definitive can be said about such a chaotic situation. Indeed, it might invite outside intervention, leading to the rapid recovery of some regions under foreign economic auspices.

[16] This assumes average annual growth of about 9 percent per year.

[17] This is not the interdependence argument of Gorbachev for a "single economic space." Most of that interdependence is economically irrational and needs to be broken for market based recovery to take place.

[18] To the extent that this gives the government political leverage to make the necessary painful changes, it does have a useful role to play. The degree to which that is so must be carefully calculated.

3

The National Question

ROMAN SZPORLUK

T he breakup of the Soviet Union and the rise of independent
states in its place have proceeded faster and further than the
replacement of Soviet political, social, and economic institutions—
or the actual changeover of the ruling elites—in any of those new
states. This alone would suggest the need for an examination of the
state of the national question in the former Soviet Union. What
are the nature and scope of nationality and nationalism there?
What is the significance of the nationality factor? What is its role in
the Soviet Union's largest successor state, the Russian Federation?

Within these basic questions, there are still other important top-
ics. Where does nationalism stand on such issues as market economy and Western-style democracy? What is its likely impact on

ROMAN SZPORLUK is M.S. Hrushevs'kyj Professor of Ukrainian History at Harvard University. From 1965 to 1991 he taught East European
history at the University of Michigan, where he also served as director of
the Center for Russian and East European Studies from 1986 to 1991. He
is widely published in the area of East European history and Soviet nationality problems. He is the author of *Communism and Nationalism: Karl
Marx versus Friedrich List.*

economic and political trends within key Soviet republics and on
fundamental questions of social class and equality? And what
range of problems is likely to be raised for the relations among the
new states, and for the outside world, by ethnic developments?

The Nationalities in the Soviet State

At the time of Gorbachev's coming to power in 1985, the USSR
consisted of fifteen "union republics," which were officially designated as sovereign socialist states, all constitutionally equal. It had
been founded in 1922, when a treaty was signed by representatives
of Russia, Ukraine, Belarus, and the Transcaucasus Federation.
Subsequently, Kazakhstan, Kyrgyzstan, Tajikistan, Turkmenistan, and Uzbekistan were separated from the Russian Soviet Fed-
erated Socialist Republic (RSFSR) and raised to the rank of union
republics. The Transcaucasus Federation was divided into
Georgia, Armenia, and Azerbaijan, and these too became constituent republics of the USSR. In 1940, Latvia, Lithuania, and
Estonia, as well as the formerly Rumanian Moldova were annexed
by Stalin and organized as union republics within the USSR. (Between 1940 and 1956 Karelia also enjoyed union republic status as
the Karelian-Finnish SSR.)

The most important union republic at all times was the RSFSR,
which occupied about 75 percent of the country's territory and had
more than half of its population. Within the Russian republic there
were more than twenty autonomous republics, autonomous districts, and other territorial units that were named after one or
another ethnic group. Union republics, autonomous republics, autonomous regions, and so forth had one thing in common—they
were considered national homelands of peoples after whom they
were named. Several very important features of Soviet nationalities policy emerged in the 1920s. First, the territory of the state was
divided into smaller units according to the ethnic composition of
the population though not always in strict conformity with it. Second, ethnicity was linked to political structure and to territory.
Third, the Soviet political and administrative system from the very
start provided for an unequal status of the component peoples of
the USSR, since their home areas were of differing ranks. Finally,

besides those nationalities that had republics and other territories
named after them, the USSR was inhabited by millions of people
belonging to dozens of ethnic groups that lacked any such territorial recognition. Those peoples included, by the post-1945 period,
Germans, Poles, Hungarians, Koreans, and others. Needless to
say, many Soviet citizens lived in republics other than those officially designated as their homelands: Russians and Ukrainians in
Kazakhstan, Armenians in Georgia, and the like.

Communism and the National Question

Legally, the Soviet Union was a federal state consisting of the
fifteen sovereign republics mentioned above. In reality it was a
highly centralized polity, and the Communist party of the Soviet
Union, which functioned as the guarantor of the state's unity, did
not even formally recognize the federal principle in its internal
organization. The party had territorial subdivisions corresponding
to republic boundaries, but the republics' Central Committees
were simply regional organizations of one party, not policy-making bodies for their respective republic organizations.

It may appear strange that the first state to be founded by followers of Karl Marx as a dictatorship of the proletariat, and intended to introduce an international Communist society, should
have been organized as a federation of ethnically or nationally
defined republics. Why was this so? The matter is much too complicated for an adequate explanation here. We simply note that
while the Communists in their view of politics and society treated
the "ethnic factor" as an aspect of class relations (nationalities
were seen as a petty bourgeois phenomenon), they created the
republics in order to facilitate Communist rule in what had been a
multiethnic state under the tsars. Lenin expected that the major
non-Russian peoples of the former Russian empire would be more
receptive to the teachings of communism if they were granted
formal statehood recognizing their equality with Russia, and if all
peoples, large and small alike, were allowed to use their native
languages in the public sphere, especially education. Lenin also
thought that the organization of the USSR as a federal, multina-
tional state would serve as a model to the rest of the world, helping

to win over to the Communist side all those dissatisfied with capitalism not only for economic or class reasons, but because capitalism condoned national or racial persecution.

What the Soviets did not consider when the Soviet Union was being founded was that their grant of linguistic autonomy and recognition of the national-territorial principle in the state's administration might prove to be disruptive in the future. Several decades ago Richard Pipes noted the importance of language and territory for the national consciousness of the peoples of the Russian Empire, especially those with some experience of independence during the revolution. He commented that "this purely formal feature of the Soviet Constitution may well prove to have been historically one of the most consequential aspects of the formation of the Soviet Union."[1]

That is precisely what became clear in the 1980s. Throughout the entire duration of the regime, the formal structure of the Soviet state reflected the *nationalist* principle according to which nations are defined by culture (especially language) and states are supposed to correspond to those cultural and linguistic features. With Gorbachev's *glasnost* these forms, which the Communists never took seriously, became revitalized as vehicles for nationalist expression. The nationalists took the Communists at their word and invoked the Soviet Constitution against those who had made it.

What Nationalism Is

Before we turn to the Soviet state's final confrontation with nationalism, let us say a word or two about what nationalism is. One scholar of the subject has written that "it is not the ethnic groups that disrupt national unity, but the perceived absence of national unity . . . that creates ethnic groups."[2] Perhaps "creates" is too strong a word: "activates politically" would be more appropriate for the Soviet case. A "nationality problem" had existed throughout the entire Soviet era, and some at least of the largest ethnic groups had qualified as full-fledged nations before Gorbachev's time. Even so, the nationality factor as a *mass* phenomenon became disruptive of the political unity of the "Soviet people," and began to function as a vehicle for the rejection of the Soviet system, at a very special historical juncture. This happened when it was becoming increasingly evident that the Soviet system had failed to build a sense of unity around the goals and the promise of communism.

Discarding the record of the Stalinist era, it is possible to grant that if Khrushchev's great challenge to the West—the new Communist party program of 1961, the last expression of Utopian belief in the superiority of communism over capitalism—had been at least a partial success, if the Soviet regime had managed to provide the people of the USSR with some measure of a decent life, then a sense of a common Soviet identity might have arisen. There would have been nationalities and nationalists, to be sure. But the nationalities as a mass would not have risen against Moscow the way they did in the 1980s, and of course the Soviet crisis would not have been there to give them a chance. Speaking in more realistic terms than Khrushchev, a reasonably successful economic reform under Gorbachev might conceivably have prevented the emergence of a mass-scale nationalist challenge to Moscow's rule in Ukraine. Even less probably would an anti-Soviet *Russian* nationalism have risen without a growing realization that not only Gorbachev but the October Revolution itself had failed to deliver on *its* promises. In sum, the rise of popular political nationalisms in the republics must be seen in connection with, and as a reaction to, the failure of "Sovietism" broadly defined.

The well-established nations of the Baltics would have been harder to satisfy even in the event of a successful Soviet system, but even they might not have rejected all forms of association with a prosperous polity that included Russia and other Soviet republics. The Baltic elites had been systematically excluded from decision making in Soviet politics, an exclusion continued under Gorbachev, and this surely was a factor in their desire for independence. As Colin Williams, following Dov Ronen's argument, points out, nationality factors such as language, religion, or race lead to nationalism when there "emerges a strong perception of an outgroup threat, the awareness of 'them'."[3] Moscow viewed the Balts as "them"; in response, the Balts concluded that they had better become fully independent.

There is nothing particularly novel in those geographers' reflections on what nationalism is about. John Stuart Mill said something of the kind in different words in the 1860s when he reflected on nationality and the state. Mill insisted that in any state that is to survive there must be "something which is settled, something permanent, and not to be called in question; . . . when the questioning of these fundamental principles is . . . the habitual condition of the body politic . . . the state is virtually in a position of civil war. . . ."[4] The condition the English philosopher spoke about is a fair description of the USSR under Gorbachev. Nationalism is a call to people to agree on constituting that unit of political organization within which they shall live and within which all their important problems will be attended to. The critical point is precisely about defining and agreeing who *is* "us" and who is "them," and on this issue the nationalists themselves differ profoundly.

Another point worth making on nationalism, and its meaning in the Soviet context especially, is that "nationalism is always a struggle for control of land" and that nation is "nothing if not a mode of constructing and interpreting social space."[5] In other words, nationalism and "ethnic politics" of the American variety are very different things.

Another perspective on nationalism, its message and its power, is provided by Alain Touraine, the distinguished sociologist and the author, among other works, of a study of the Solidarity movement in Poland in 1980–81. For Touraine Solidarity signaled the end of communism by setting forth "an alternative agenda of historical action." Perhaps the same can be said about the role of nationality and nationalism in the breakup of the Soviet system, and about the prospects of nationalism in a post-Communist world. Following Touraine, we can look at national identity "in terms of choice and not in terms of substance, essence or tradition," and recognize in it "a claim to a capacity for action and for change." Those struggling to create a new identity are trying "to determine for themselves the conditions within which their collective and personal life is produced."[6]

Touraine's comments are especially valuable because much contemporary writing about the nature of nation and nationalism in the Soviet Union and its successor states remains deeply permeated by assumptions of European nineteenth century nationalist thought, and many writers (Western and ex-Soviet alike) appear to be unaware of this legacy in their own arguments. For example, nationalism in the 1800s argued that "states" should correspond to "nations" that were defined by linguistic or cultural criteria. Historians, of course, have always known that even at the time when nationalist sentiments enjoyed the greatest influence, virtually no state qualified as culturally homogeneous in the nationalist understanding of the term. But the language of nationalism was unequivocal on this matter, and governments and political movements invoked the nationalist argument when it suited them. Equally strongly, they ignored or rejected it when it did not. The post-1918 story of self-determination of nations in Eastern Europe and peacemaking supposedly based on this principle is well known. And yet it is not uncommon now to read analyses in which the fact of this-or-that Soviet republic's this-or-that region being ethnically different from the rest of the said republic is presented as an anomaly, a problem that requires an explanation, if not a call for an immediate rectification. Calls for border revisions are understandable when they come from sides involved in national conflicts. They should be viewed, however, as partisan political positions (conscious or unconscious), not as neutral, "scientific" statements about facts, and as such they do not belong in scholarly analysis.

Another residue of nationalism in today's thinking is to treat nations as entities with fixed, permanent characteristics and with easily determined membership. In the past three or four decades most Western scholarship on nationalism has abandoned this reification of nations. Nations, as Touraine and other specialists now agree, are constantly redefining themselves, making and remaking their identities. It is a banal thing to say that the French were being made and remade long after 1789, which, earlier generations were sure, had settled the French question once and for all. Stalin's writings on the nationality question reveal this earlier understanding of how "in the West" nations had supposedly taken shape, forever, long ago. Today he would have been surprised to hear of the Basques or Catalonia, not to mention Nagorno-Karabakh or Northern Ireland.

The post-Soviet scene can be better understood if one sees it as a full-scale debate—and a fierce political struggle—about the making, remaking, and unmaking of political identities, nations, and states. Moreover, it is important to see nationality not only as a problem but also as a solution. To be precise, in the collapse of the Soviet regime one ought to see not merely Communist failures, including the Communist "failure to solve the national question," but a victory of nationalist programs, ones consciously designed as an alternative to the Soviet system, i.e., "national *answers*." The Soviet Union may have collapsed, but a new Russia, a Russia professing its adherence to democracy and liberty and one that Russian democrats had failed to establish in 1917, has risen as the USSR's largest and most powerful successor. Other nations, some of which had never before been free of foreign rule, are also trying to build independent states. Thus while Soviet loyalists at home (and many observers abroad) describe the post-Soviet scene in the words "The King is dead," there are many others happy to add: "Long live the King!" For them, history is only beginning.

The victory of the nationalist alternative to communism should not at the same time make us dismiss a priori all the other potential outcomes of the Soviet crisis that existed prior to the breakup. After all, many shrewd observers, in the USSR and abroad, contemplated other possible futures for the Soviet Union after communism: a democratic and liberal system, a renewed socialist society, an authoritarian regime with military in (or sharing) power, and so on. The only concession that most of them made to nationalism was to allow the possibility of the Baltic republics seceding. In the end nationalism succeeded in preempting all those alternatives to communism that were predicated on the retention of a single state within the borders of the USSR. There is no need to belabor the obvious point, that the victory of nationalism does not by itself signify a victory of Western democracy. National independence is only the first article of nationalist faith. Nationalisms differ from one another on questions of political and social organization, on economy and culture, and they even disagree on the definition of such central concepts as the nation for which they claim to speak. The successor states of the USSR are facing all these questions, and each is doing it in its own idiom and in its own way.

Gorbachev versus the Republics

Gorbachev's agenda was only marginally concerned with nationality matters. Indeed there is clear evidence that he hoped gradually to diminish the importance of the republics and the nationality factor altogether as the Soviet Union moved away from Stalinist practices and evolved in new directions. Some scholars have even spoken, when referring to Gorbachev's early policies, of his "running against the republics." On the other hand, the nationalities, especially those with the higher status of union republics, gradually, and with increasing force, made it clear that they wanted to raise and broaden the powers they enjoyed and to weaken correspondingly the powers enjoyed by the Kremlin. They had very different aspirations and solutions than those favored by Gorbachev and his associates.

In Gorbachev's time the very nature and meaning of the nationality question was the subject of stubborn struggle. On the one hand, Gorbachev and the Soviet establishment sought the downgrading of the "nationality question" to the level of an "ethnic" minority-rights question—one of the many specific and secondary problems Soviet society had to deal with as it was preoccupied with the fundamental task of *perestroika*. In this overall scheme, accordingly, they insisted that the rights of ethnic minorities *within* the union republics were to be protected by the center. They also favored a de facto elevation of the autonomous republics to the status of union republics, which was another way to weaken the union republics' traditional and constitutional special status. In some pronouncements reflecting the center's position, all Soviet nationalities, regardless of their size and administrative-political status, were to be equal, as were all Soviet citizens. The rights of individuals, regardless of their ethnic identity and place of residence, were to be protected throughout the state, that is, the USSR; to secure these rights, USSR authorities were to be assigned a position of superiority over the republics.

One might say that Moscow wanted to treat the needs of the nationalities like those of juveniles, the handicapped, or other categories of people with special requirements or specific characteristics: to provide special facilities for their exercise of their rights, to give them special arrangements in matters of access to education, radio and TV, and so forth. All of this was to be done, to repeat, under the authority of central all-union law and all-union law-enforcing agencies. What Gorbachev completely failed to grasp is that once aroused, the nationalist movements represented a new vision of political space and national organization, and not simply a movement analogous to, say, the civil rights movement in the United States in the 1960s, which accepted, indeed invoked, the supremacy of the United States Constitution. His failure to understand that Nagorno-Karabakh was a conflict over land and power is a perfect illustration of his misjudgment of the nationalist agendas.

Nationalism against the Center

On the opposite side in this dispute stood the national movements of the union republics and some of the autonomous republics. They presented their demands first in the Baltic republics, but gradually their concerns were adopted by others. The nationalists in the Baltics and elsewhere invoked the sovereign rights of their states, the constitutional prerogatives of the union republics that only the union republics enjoyed, most important of which was the constitutional right freely to secede from the USSR. This kind of nationalism transformed the "nationality question" into a matter of relations between sovereign states and placed their relations with "the center," as it tended to be known, in a completely different perspective.

When the nationalists challenged Moscow, they did so not by proposing an alternative to the leaders or policies at the center, but by creating a vision of an altogether different territory—a national homeland—and a different form of its organization. In other words, they engaged in the work of a "national construction of social space." Thus from their point of view nationalism was not a problem; it was a *solution,* or a different way of approaching the problems of Soviet society and politics.

In brief, if Gorbachev and the center wanted to downgrade or "ethnicize" the national question, the alternative view in the republics transformed it into a question of relations between states—it *étatized* and *internationalized* the nationality question.

The controversy over a new treaty of union was thus a struggle of these two conceptions of nationality. Gorbachev and his supporters wanted to allow as many nationalities as possible, and at least the nationalities of the autonomous republics, to become the signatories of the treaty, i.e., "subjects of the union," and they also wanted the representatives of the center to become a party to that treaty. On the opposing side were those who defended the exclusive right of the sovereign union republics, as the sole proprietors of their space, to participate in any such accords. They explicitly denied the center any right to be a participant.

It is now clear why after 1985 the national question became the defining question of all issues of importance in the Soviet Union, and how interethnic relations came to be transformed into international relations. After the Ukrainian popular vote for independence on December 1, 1991, all-union agencies were dissolved, and thus "internationalization" of Soviet politics was formally recognized both within the former USSR and by the international community. The USSR ceased to exist. Gorbachev rightly insisted in his final statements as president of the USSR (December 3 and December 18, 1991) that the real crisis of the USSR was the crisis of statehood (*gosudarstvennost*). He seemed to have finally grasped that the fundamental dividing line in "Soviet" politics was between those who accepted the USSR as a state, on the one hand, and those who did not, and who regarded their nations and republics as sovereign actors, the only legitimate units of social and political organization of their territories.

The New Russian Agenda

Perhaps the most damaging blow to the cause of saving the integrity of the USSR came from Russia. Russian anti-Soviet nationalism existed ever since 1917, but for many decades there were good reasons to consider that this type of nationalism was much weaker than was Soviet Russian nationalism. Indeed, well into the Gorbachev era some leading experts on the Soviet Union took for granted a complete fusion of "Sovietism" with "Russianness," so to say, and they used the adjectives "Russian" and "Soviet" interchangeably, as synonyms.[7] But by that time a wide spectrum of anti-Soviet Russian nationalist views was in evidence.

In an article written in 1989, I discussed the "dilemmas of Russian nationalism," arguing that Russian nationalism could be divided into two basic currents. Would Russian national consciousness define itself through an identification with the empire—this was the camp of "empire savers"—or would there emerge an alternative geographical model of Russia, a Russia as a nation-state? Those advocating the latter, who had different visions of Russia as a nation-state, were called "nation builders."[8]

Much has changed since the summer of 1989. A Russia emerged that defined itself distinctly from, and in opposition to, Gorbachev's "center." The elections of 1990 produced a Russian parliament, those of 1991, a Russian president. The empire no longer exists, even though the Soviet Union's first and last president insisted until the very end on identifying the country he presided over with what he called a thousand-year-old state. Thus for Gorbachev the USSR was identical with Russia and that Russia was defined in imperial terms. The new Russia does not define itself in those terms, but finds it very difficult to shape its identity on an alternative basis.

Boris Yeltsin, who in mid-1989 had not yet adopted the Russian republic as his political stage, but who owes his rise to his playing the Russian card, has given many indications that he prefers a nonimperial Russia. This stand is especially clearly expressed in his position on Ukrainian sovereignty, which he recognized as early as November 1990. The vice president of Russia, Alexander Rutskoi, on the other hand, remains the most articulate and the most highly placed defender of the idea of continuity between old imperial and post-Soviet Russia. He is calling for a restoration of the old state under a new name, and he insists that the Russian Federation and the "real" Russia that includes the other ex-Soviet republics are different entities.[9] There are many others in Russia who hold an even stronger view on this issue. One inevitably asks how much depends on the personalities of individual leaders at such historical junctures. Should Yeltsin leave office, for whatever reasons, what will the consequences be for Russia, Russian-Ukrainian relations, Russian-Tatar relations, and so on?

Those who insist on Russia's being something larger than the
Russian Federation have Ukraine especially in mind as a part of
that larger Russia. The Russian-Ukrainian dispute over the Black
Sea Fleet, and the arguments over who is the proper owner of the
Crimea, are really issues about the fundamental question: is
Ukraine a nation in its own right, or is it a part of Russia? Even
Alexander Solzhenitsyn, as we know, remains convinced that the
latter is the case, and he presents the history of Ukrainian national-
ism in accordance with this position.[10] In post-Soviet Russian poli-
tics some voices are heard calling not only for the "return" of
Ukraine to Russia but also for the restoration of Russian rule in the
Baltic states and even in Finland. But one does not have to be a
Russian chauvinist to find the new geography of Russia hard to
accept. As Stanislav Kondrashov points out, the independence of
the Baltic states, Belarus, and Ukraine pushes Russia farther away
from Europe. Having been—as the USSR—a neighbor of Poland,
Czechoslovakia, and Hungary in the west, Russia now is separated
from Europe by the Baltic states and Ukraine and Belarus![11]

The issues Russia faces as it takes shape after communism are
many. The Russia-Ukraine problem is fundamental in post-Soviet
ethnic politics because it concerns the two largest nations and
because the way it is resolved will influence the fate of others as
well. But there are many other issues within the Russian Federation. Russia's internal nationality problems belong to several distinct types and require different solutions. First, there are territorial nations whose status until recent years had been that of
autonomous republics but who have since redefined themselves as
sovereign nation-states. They include Tatarstan, Bashkorstan,
Yakutia, Tuva, and Chechen-Ingushetia. The most serious among
these is the movement for independence in Tatarstan. The so-
called Volga Tatars, with a capital in Kazan, were conquered by
Russia in the sixteenth century. Their separation would break
Russia into two parts, European and Asian, and the very idea of
such an outcome is unthinkable to virtually all Russians. Relations
between Russia and Tatarstan became a central question for
Russia after 1991. Next, there are smaller nationalities asking for a
measure of territorial autonomy inside a reformed Russia, but
definitely not seeking full independence. Russia also has minorities

lacking at present a territorial-state recognition but pressing for such recognition—most notably, the Germans. Finally, there are many people in Russia whose historic homelands are located outside the Russian Federation and who are now independent. They include several million Ukrainians, who will be satisfied with cultural rights in Russia but are otherwise not asking even for regional autonomy. The way Russia treats "its" Ukrainians will bear on the condition of ethnic Russians in Ukraine, and both will be influenced by the interstate relations of Ukraine and Russia.

Some of the minority questions of Russia have external ramifications extending beyond the former USSR: they include the already mentioned Germans, first of all, but also Koreans, Poles, and Finns. To this category of problems also belongs the "Jewish question." For many Russians the Jews belong to a special category of "internal-cum-external" problems. While many individuals of Jewish descent are for all purposes Russian and consider themselves as such, their admission, as it were, to full-fledged membership in the Russian nation is being challenged by certain conceptions of Russian nationality even while it is being accepted by others. For some Russians, Russian Orthodoxy is the marker of Russian nationality. This, in turn, does not only exclude Jews, Protestants, or atheists, but bears on one's view of Russia's relation to the outside world. Those who accept a secular definition of Russian identity are likely to favor a Western-style form of government, and a "Western" economic system for Russia. Those who believe that only the Orthodox, or at least only Christians, can be truly Russian question the national credentials of millions of current Russian citizens and declare themselves against Western institutions and values.

While it is easy for the non-Russians to convince themselves that the Revolution of 1917 and the system it created were "foreign," something imposed on them by "Moscow" or "Russia," it is much harder to demonstrate convincingly that the October Revolution was "un-Russian." It is not necessary to agree with Stalin's dictum that "Leninism is the highest achievement of Russian culture" to recognize the *Russian* roots of Bolshevism and the Soviet system. However, many Russians, especially Solzhenitsyn, deny the "Russian" character of 1917: they see it as a *break* with Russia.

For decades the official ideology tried to identify Russia with communism. Now, after the fall of communism, those who view Russia as a part of Europe tend to accept the view that "capitalism" is compatible with Russia's national spirit or character. Those who view Russia as a world apart—"Eurasia"—are inclined to seek a new solution for Russia, a third way between capitalism and socialism, or try to find some even less clear, special "Russian" economic and social way of life. The "Eurasian" vision of Russia may not be the most popular one in contemporary Russia, but it does define "Eurasia" as both Slavic *and* Turkic, Christian *and* Muslim, Western *and* Eastern, and thus offers a formula that might in theory at least be acceptable to the Tatars, for whom a Slavic and a Christian Russia has to be an alien entity. Solzhenitsyn's prescription for Russia, while it sees Russia as a nation of Europe that differs from the West in important ways, does not offer a solution acceptable to the Tatars because he views Russia as a Slavic and Christian nation.

The question of ideology and politics as the core of Russian identity is connected, as we see, to the questions of history and geography. For many Russians, the collapse of the Soviet state is identical with an unprecedented defeat of Russia as *Russia*. Whatever one may think about the bad or good sides of communism, the defeat of communism in the USSR has come together with— some will say it has caused—the separation from Russia of lands and peoples many Russians have long believed to be theirs by virtue of Russian history prior to communism.

While for many this nostalgia after the old greater Russia has basically emotional or sentimental roots, others may have more practical reasons to invoke the old empire's glories. It is not hard to recognize that for influential and sizable social forces the breakdown of the Soviet Union has meant a professional disaster: those include the state and party bureaucracy, the industrial bureaucracy, the military, and the police. Their job had been to maintain the non-Russian peoples and republics under Moscow's control. What will they do in a Russia deprived of those "borderlands"? A recourse to Russia's imperial past serves as a useful rationale for providing themselves with a mission, not simply reclaiming their jobs.

The post-Soviet Russian problems can be summed up in the form of two pairs of alternatives. First, for the Russian Federation as it is now constituted, the central question is whether the political nation of Russia will consist of all citizens of the republic, regardless of their ethnic, linguistic, religious, or racial background, or will the Russian nation be synonymous with ethnic Russians alone. It goes without saying that the decision as to whether a political definition of the nation of Russia is adopted depends on the willingness of both Russians and non-Russians to do so. Such an agreement would create a favorable ethnic climate for the establishment of a democratic government in Russia, while the ethnic option would make a democracy difficult, if not impossible.

There is also the problem of ethnically *Russian* regions of Russia. Even when the Russians agree about what Russia is and who is Russian, they remain deeply divided on how the Russian state should be subdivided administratively and territorially. Should the ethnically Russian regions of the Russian republic also enjoy a degree of autonomy? Should Russia be a federation of (nonethnic) lands modeled on Germany, for example, or on the United States or Canada? Russia extends from the Baltic to the Pacific, and the Far East, Siberia, the Urals, and the St. Petersburg region, to name a few, can legitimately call for administrative autonomy, regardless of any ethnic considerations.

The second question is about what *is* the real Russia: is the Russian Federation equal to Russia, or is Russia—the "real Russia"—a larger entity? If the latter is the case, the question arises whether those "Russian" lands outside the Russian Federation should be considered a *Russia irredenta*, and the Russians living there a real or potential fifth column, waiting for their *Anschluss* to Russia. This view is clearly the position of those people in Moscow (and in the West) who are finding it intolerable that the Crimea is a part of the Republic of Ukraine. (It appears that most Russians actually living in the Crimea find their present situation less intolerable than some of their defenders are doing in Moscow or Washington, D.C.) The dispute over the Crimea may be best understood as having its origin in two mutually opposed concepts of nationhood and citizenship. One concept maintains that the political nation should be coextensive with the cultural nationality, especially with the language community. Accordingly, it sees Russians living in countries other than Russia as living abroad, as foreigners in those countries, even if they enjoy the citizenship of those countries. Furthermore, it holds that when those Russians living in a foreign country form a compact group, and constitute a majority in a region or a locality, they have the right to join Russia—together with their territory—thereby seceding from the state that they are citizens of, but consider foreign.

The idea of an ethnic nation, as we shall see, is upheld in many other parts of the former Soviet Union. What makes it especially explosive in the Russian case is the size of the Russian population and the importance of the Russian Federation in the constellation of post-Soviet states. In a real sense, the Russian Federation is another Soviet Union. The Russian question today arguably can be compared in importance to the German question in the nineteenth and first half of the twentieth century. The similarities in the old German and current Russian national problems are indeed striking. For German nationalists even before Hitler, but for Hitler especially, all ethnic Germans, regardless of their citizenship, and regardless of their residence, were a part of the German nation. The current Russian discussions regarding the status of Russians in Ukraine, Kazakhstan, or Belarus bring to mind Germany's relations with Czechoslovakia and Austria after 1918.

The Remaking of Ukraine

If Russia today in some respects resembles Germany of sixty years ago, Ukraine bears a close similarity to the pre-1938 Czechoslovakia with its intractable Czecho-Slovak dualism and especially with its 3-million strong German mass, comprising about the same share of Czechoslovakia's population as the Russians do in today's Ukraine. A modern Ukrainian political nation is currently being made. The outcome is still uncertain. Ukraine's relations with Russia will unquestionably influence the process of nation building in Ukraine and will especially have an impact on how Russian-Ukrainian relations develop in the Ukrainian republic.

The leadership of Ukraine argues that the national identity of the people of Ukraine is based not on ethnic or linguistic criteria, but on a political criterion, the community of *citizenship*. In conformity with this "statist" or political definition of Ukrainian identity, the Russians of Ukraine are officially regarded as fully rightful Ukrainian citizens who happen to speak Russian. In other words, state building rather than nation building is the key slogan, and the emphasis is on civic and political, not ethnic and cultural, markers of the community. Such is the official line of President Leonid Kravchuk, and it appears also to be advocated by his (former) opponents from the democratic and nationalist camp. Whether this concept becomes the operating principle in reality will depend on two factors: the self-restraint of the traditional Ukrainian nationalists, for whom language and culture were the principal criteria of nationality, and the willingness of Russia to respect the territorial integrity of a Ukraine containing millions of Russian speakers.

Historical traditions will also play a role, although the process and outcome will be determined by more immediate circumstances. The most important historical factor to consider is that Ukraine, like the Baltic states and unlike the republics of Central Asia, does have a non-Soviet past as a political entity. Forms of a Ukrainian statehood existed at the time of the revolution of 1917 in Russia, and in the West in the former Austrian province of Galicia. The Ukrainian People's Republic of 1917–18, the Ukrainian state under Helmet Pavlo Skoropadsky in 1918, and the West Ukrainian People's Republic of 1918–19 not only aspired to be independent but also professed their adherence to the idea that Ukraine was a common country for all its people. However, they were never able to make this ideal a reality because their existence was measured in months, not years, and none ever enjoyed the conditions of peace. The creation of a Soviet Ukraine by Moscow can be directly linked to Lenin's recognition of the appeal of Ukrainian nationalism. Twenty years later, the annexation of the western regions of Ukraine, which Stalin carried out in 1939, 1940, and 1945, was legitimized by him in Ukrainian nationalist terms as "reunification of all Ukrainian lands in a single Soviet Ukrainian state." Whatever Stalin's real motives, the events of 1939–45 popularized the idea of a Ukrainian state. Those western regions had diverse and contradictory traditions, and their pre-Soviet experience with de

mocracy was more extensive than that of any other part of the
Soviet Union except the Baltic states.

In the 1960s a Ukrainian national movement emerged in the
USSR that was both national and democratic, and one of its most
lasting intellectual legacies was the idea that all citizens of Ukraine
should enjoy full rights, regardless of ethnic origins, religion, or
race. That tradition was revived by the political movements of the
late 1980s and early 1990s. Some of the dissidents of the 1960s
reemerged among the newly elected political leaders. The concept
of *narod Ukrainy,* "the people of Ukraine," is hence a genuine element of an indigenous tradition, not a tactical device intended to
dupe Ukraine's Russians into passivity.

Let us repeat, however, that Ukraine has also had quite different
traditions in its history, including an ethnic definition of Ukrainian
nationality. At present ethnocentric and xenophobic views do not
enjoy great popularity in Ukraine and do not form a significant
element of contemporary political consciousness. If the model of a
political and territorial Ukraine promoted by the current Ukrainian leadership fails, we can expect an ethnic definition of Ukrainian nationality to be revived together with an "ethnicization" of
the Russian-speaking inhabitants of Ukraine, thereby resulting in
a breakup of Ukraine along language lines. It is essential to stress
that Kravchuk and Co. are challenging the old Ukrainian nationalist ideas, and are in fact building a new Ukrainian identity, just as
they are posing a challenge to Russian ideas on Ukraine. Under
Ukraine's present conditions this appears to be the optimal way
"to redefine space and to reconstruct the environment as a distinctly political territory," which is what all nation and state builders aspire to do.[12]

Considering that Ukraine as a "political territory" is very new,
its present boundaries having been established in 1939–45 (with
the Crimea added in 1954), it is evident that those aspiring to
create an independent Ukrainian state in a peaceful and democratic way, that is, with the consent of the people, have had to face
a number of issues in the area of integrating those people in a
political space. Here are some of those potentially disruptive issues:

1. the ethnic fault line between Ukrainians and non-Ukrainians, Russians, in particular;

2. divisions between Ukrainian-speaking Ukrainians and those speaking Russian (although declaring their Ukrainian nationality in the census);

3. religious differences between Ukrainians of Orthodox faith and those of Catholic faith;

4. political and social differences between those areas that became Soviet only in 1939–45 and those that had already been Soviet in the 1920s and 1930s;

5. the conflict between Communists and anti-Communists, including nationalist victims of Communist repression.

Looking from a somewhat different perspective, the contemporary Ukraine clearly faces the problem of creating and sustaining a common identity that would bring together the traditionally agricultural west and the industrial and urban east and southeast. This territorial dualism in Ukraine, which roughly corresponds to the linguistic divisions of Ukraine—Ukrainian west, Russian east— can be approached in still another way: the east and the south in the social/occupational composition of their population are predominantly working class, with a sizable component of engineering and technical personnel. It is not self-evident a priori why these people should decide to cast their lot—to define themselves politically—with a Ukraine, and conclude that their ties to Ukraine are more important than is their professional solidarity with their fellow workers and engineers in Russia.

On the other hand, there are certain socioeconomic factors that work in favor of Ukrainian unity within the present borders. Even though the east is conventionally described as Russian (I did this above), many of those "Russians" are Ukrainian by descent and consider themselves Ukrainian. Their national identity remains rather fluid. There also exists a working class speaking Ukrainian in the west and in central regions, and there is little evidence of an ethnic division of labor suggesting a pattern of "internal colonialism." Ukrainians do occupy managerial positions, and have been

sufficiently represented in the party machine to cast into doubt any
attempts to represent Ukrainians as a socially exploited nationality. Moreover, the industrial level of the east is no longer an index
of its modernity. Even in the former Soviet Union it is generally
acknowledged that Soviet industry belongs really to the nineteenth
century. Ukraine's east, which for decades served in Soviet propa-
ganda as a proof of the superiority of the city over the village, is
now viewed as a serious problem. Paradoxically, the "backward"
west is free of the handicaps of the east—and happens to be at a
close proximity to Europe, and thus the capitalist world.

These facts may have played a role in persuading the miners of
the Donbass region that opting for Kiev rather than Moscow
would be beneficial, or at least less risky, if not for them, then for
their children. Chernobyl, and the growing realization that practically the entire Ukraine is an ecological disaster area, contributed
to a sense of common danger and fate.

With these problems in mind, the political events of 1989–91
may be viewed as building blocks in the creation of a political
coalition that tried to integrate Ukraine above all these fault lines.
The party-state machinery of the old regime, or at least its more
flexible part, on the one hand, and the newly emergent nationalist
and democratic forces, on the other, gradually discovered a community of interests. The ex-Communist party activists, of course,
represent the east, whereas the democratic nationalists owed their
election to the Soviet and Ukrainian parliaments, and thus their
entry into politics, mainly to the constituencies located in the western regions.

The Ukrainian parliament became the body where the Communists and nationalists learned to work together. The previously
unknown political talents of Kravchuk were revealed first, and
most strikingly, in his role as chairman of the Ukrainian Supreme
Soviet. One of his master strokes was to co-opt the nationalists by
awarding them many more committee chairs than their numerical
size in the parliament justified. There was also a redefinition of the
political agenda itself—but most of all, a change in the language,
the language of political geography. Another move was to allow a
"Ukrainian" question in the Gorbachev referendum of March
1991, and to permit a third question in the western regions of

Galicia. As Kravchuk said himself, the inclusion of these questions made it possible to avoid violent protests in the most dangerous spots. Instead of mass campaigns for a boycott of the vote, those who did not like the language proposed by Gorbachev were able to answer questions to their liking by going to the ballot box. It is impossible to determine how much the relative stability of Ukraine, the absence of anti-Communist witchhunts, the moderation of the nationalist forces, the prevention of violence in the Catholic-Orthodox disputes, the politics of coalition building in Kiev—how much all of these are to be attributed to the personal leadership skills of Kravchuk. Would any other leader have done so well?

The decision to declare Ukraine's sovereignty in July 1990 came barely one month after a similar declaration by Russia. The declaration of independence of August 1991 was a direct response to the coup and cited the coup in its text as the reason why Ukraine had to become independent. Finally, the decision to hold a referendum on December 1, 1991, was a compromise between the party and nationalist forces. The results came as a surprise to all. Here again events in Moscow played a role: Gorbachev's direct involvement in the campaign, and the engagement of the Moscow media in the campaign, according to many observers, helped create an anti-Moscow backlash in Ukraine. These initial steps in the building of a Ukraine seem to have been quite successful. But the agenda is long, and the question of economic reform cannot be avoided by patriotic appeals. Just as in Russia and the other republics, success in improving people's living conditions will be a major, if not decisive, factor in determining the future of the current experiment in independence and democracy.

Were the subject of this chapter an academic discussion of nationality problems in the former Soviet Union, it would have been proper to charge that it devotes a disproportionate amount of attention to the problems of Russia and Ukraine at the expense of smaller nationalities. For, indeed, to the student of nationality the numerical size or political importance of a people in question is not the primary concern. The emphasis of this chapter, however, is on policy-relevant problems. Therefore, it is quite evident that the two largest nations merit a special degree of attention. This is also true about their relationship. How it develops will determine the fate of not only Russians or Ukrainians. The outcome of the crisis over the Black Sea Fleet, the question of the Crimea, the fate of reform in Russia will all have an impact on the processes of nation building in Ukraine, and internal Ukrainian developments will reciprocally influence nation building and democratic reform in Russia. If the Crimea becomes another Nagorno-Karabakh, the crisis will have repercussions exceeding by far the impact of the tragic events in the Caucasus. We shall now turn to other regions of the ex–Soviet Union for a look at their ways of dealing with nationality and nationalism.

Civil Society or Civil War?
Varieties of Nationalist Experience

In the former union republics of the Soviet Union today, "nationalism" has become a concern with, and perhaps an "ideology" of, state building and nation building within a newly independent state. Within each such new state competing models of state and nation are being promoted and tested. As our discussion of Russia showed, one of the aspects of nation building involves solving the question of "national geography." The new nations ask such questions as: are "we" a part of Europe? What do we mean by "Europe"? Or: do we belong to the Islamic world? Are we Asian? . . .

Another nationalist question, a particularly important one in the present post-Communist crisis, concerns what the correct *national* position should be on market economy, private property, free trade, protectionism, and, most urgently, on the question of citizenship and political rights and institutions in general. Unlike the Russians, for whom the issue of Russian roots of communism is much more problematic, the non-Russian nationalities view communism as foreign and identify its fall with their national liberation from Russia. It seems that for this reason they may find it easier, at least in the European republics, to convince themselves that "capitalism" corresponds to their national tradition and is likely to help them to "return to Europe." In the immediate post-Soviet period, the former European republics are defining themselves in "Euro-

pean" and "promarket" terms. The three Transcaucasus republics are also declaring themselves for "Europe." In ex–Soviet Asia
the picture is less clear.

In the ethnic heterogeneity of their populations, not only Russia
and Ukraine, whose multiethnic character is evident, but virtually
all the republics are smaller-scale replicas of the old Soviet Union.
If they prove successful in dealing with their economic reforms
(privatization) and political reforms (democracy, and human and
civil rights) the disruptive potential of ethnicity will be aborted. On
the other hand, economic failures, political difficulties, the absence
of democracy, will tend to activate ethnicity as the basis for secession. Earlier we suggested that the independence of republics was
a solution to the Soviet Union's problems. Only time will show
whether this solution will in turn avoid becoming a problem itself.

While they resemble the late USSR in their ethnic makeup, the
new states are beginning their independent life with some advantages over it. Unlike the USSR, for example, most republics are
unitary states by their formal constitution. In those states where
autonomous republics exist, however, an institutional framework
for a possible challenge to the state's integrity also exists. In other
cases, ethnic groups do not have a formal recognition as a state,
and thus lack a territorial basis for advancing their alternative
visions of economic and political organization. This does not
mean, however, that those nationalities will be deterred by such
legal considerations from pressing their claims to a statehood. The
Crimean Tatars, for example, demand self-determination (although not a complete independence) even though they lack an
autonomous republic.

Much will depend on how the majority nations of the newly
independent states will define their relationship to their minority
fellow citizens and what status they will assign to themselves in
their respective states. For example, will the solution that is being
attempted in Ukraine become dominant in all of the fifteen post-
Soviet republics? The terms "people of Ukraine," "people of Kazakhstan," or "the people of Russia" are used in the official docu-
ments of several new states. But what the realities behind these
words will be is still not clear. There are signs that some other
newly independent states, such as Georgia, and arguably also Ar-

menia, Azerbaijan, and Moldova, have a different vision of their
nationhood. They consider it their task to make their population
conform ethnically and linguistically to their political organization. To achieve this conformity, they want to use political and
administrative measures to promote an ethnic and linguistic
homogenization of their states. These measures may include linguistic assimilation, but they might also include forcible deporta-
tions of "alien" populations.

Those following this course in their state and nation building
will be repeating the policies of the new national states of East
Central Europe after 1918. In the latter, the state power was regarded as a party in the interethnic conflict within the country. To
be precise, it was treated as an instrument of the majority nation in
its struggle against "the minorities," even though these minorities
formally enjoyed the rights of citizenship along with the majority
nation. Linguistic assimilation rather than building a common citizenship, regardless of language or ethnicity, became the primary
goal of governments in such states as Poland or Rumania after
1918. Toward certain minorities the course pursued was one encouraging outright emigration or resulting in an open, "legal"
denial of rights to certain categories of citizens. The situation was
different in Czechoslovakia, which came closer than any other
new state to practicing national equality of citizens. However,
even in Czechoslovakia a distinction was made between the Cze-
choslovaks, i.e., Czechs and Slovaks, who were declared to be "the
nation of the state," and to whom that state properly belonged, on
the one hand, and "the minorities," on the other. As we know, in
the end Czechoslovakia failed to win over its German-speaking
citizens for the idea of a Czechoslovakia that would be *their* country too, and it also did not solve the conflict between the Czechs
and Slovaks. Bearing in mind those examples of past failures by
otherwise admirable leaders (who would claim that any of the
current post-Soviet leaders is superior to Thomas Masaryk?), we
may ask how realistic is the current citizenship-building program.
Will Ukraine, Kazakhstan, Belarus, Latvia, and others persuade
their ethnically Russian citizens to accept Ukraine, Kazakhstan, et
al. as their country? Will other minorities accept the status quo?

The prospects of interethnic peace will vary from region to

region, republic to republic. Somewhat schematically, we might draw the following picture of the nationality problems of the new post-Soviet states.

In the Baltic states of Estonia, Latvia, and Lithuania, the dominant approach is to identify nation with the state, and therefore no attempt is made, at least officially, to create, say, a concept of the "people of Lithuania," which would embrace Lithuania's Poles, Russians, Jews, and Ukrainians in a political nation common with ethnic Lithuanians. However, it would be a realistic goal to ask the Baltic states for recognition of the individual and group rights of the minority nationalities. In some cases—Poles in Lithuania, Russians in Estonia—minorities have asked for local territorial autonomy, but these demands do not have to lead to secession. It should be acknowledged that since Latvians and Estonians enjoy only a slim majority of their populations, they have reason to fear they may be outnumbered within their respective countries. Their situation calls for creative state-building techniques that would grant equality to all citizens.

Belarus may be at an even more delicate and precarious stage of nation building than Ukraine. The Belarusians enjoy a high numerical preponderance, but they use the Russian language even more widely than do Ukrainians in Ukraine, and a common Belarus nationality will have to extend to Russian speakers if the integrity of Belarus is to be preserved. A strong sense of territorial identity exists in Belarus, and the entire population shares in the problems and dangers caused by Chernobyl.

After the fall of the USSR, Moldova faced the choice of either joining Rumania or becoming the second Rumanian state. Relations with the non-Moldovan population, mainly Russians and Ukrainians, were extremely tense; armed clashes were frequent, and the eastern portion of the republic declared its secession as a Dniester republic. The prospects for a territorial-political nationhood were slim. Would it be possible to persuade the Russian-speaking secessionists to return to Moldova as a regular part of the state? It was not clear whether the Russians would accept a form of broad autonomy analogous to the autonomy the Crimea had in Ukraine, or whether the Moldovan state would agree to such a deal.

From 1988 on, the situation in the states of the Transcaucasus has been widely reported. The states of Armenia and Azerbaijan have been in a de facto war over Nagorno-Karabakh, and the prospects for a peaceful resolution are still not clear. A deal involving an exchange of populations might offer the most humane way out of a hopeless situation. Georgia, as noted earlier, has been engaged in a classical, pre-1939 East European–style nation-building project in which the rights of the other nationalities are seen as an obstacle to Georgian national freedom.

The situation in Kazakhstan superficially resembles the Ukrainian situation in that Russians form a compact mass of people and occupy a distinct portion of land. In Kazakhstan, however, several factors make the likelihood of a Kazakh-Russian concord problematic. First, the cultural, linguistic, and religious distance between the Kazakhs and the Russians is much more of a problem than is the case in Ukraine. In Kazakhstan there exists no category of people whose national identity is somewhere between Kazakh and Russian. To survive, Kazakhstan presumably will have to become an openly binational state rather than one professing the less realistic goal of a "Kazakhstani" nationhood embracing Kazakhs and Russians in a single nation.

The republics of Central Asia, unlike those of Europe, do not have a pre-Soviet history in which they existed as Uzbekistan, Krygyzstan, and so on. Their pre-Russian and pre-Soviet political experience is quite alien to modern concepts of nationalism. To what extent have the creations of the 1920s and 1930s acquired an authentic legitimacy in the eyes of their populations—and in those of their neighbors? Scholars on the region tend to agree that the formerly Soviet republics of Central Asia have become meaningful political entities and that their elites think and operate within the framework of their respective newly independent states. The role model, as it were, in state building for these post-Soviet elites is Turkey because it is secular, democratic, relatively "Western" and yet Muslim at the same time. But one should not exclude the possibility that under certain conditions Iran may provide an alternative model and an alternative source of support in their state-building efforts. It is another question whether the ideas of pan-Turkism, pan-Islam, and some other supranational programs will

win support in the future. Whatever happens, it is also doubtful the
Russians and other "Europeans" can expect to enjoy a role in the
independent states of Central Asia that is comparable to what the
minorities can aspire to in, say, Latvia or Estonia. We will more
likely see a continuation in the gradual exodus of Russians, Ukrainians, Jews, and other Europeans from those states to Russia,
Ukraine, or to the West (or Israel) that began several years before
the dissolution of the USSR.

Conclusions

It is very doubtful that the successor states of the Soviet Union
will agree to treat the Commonwealth of Independent States as a
structure comparable in its role and functions with the European
Community. In their foreign policy relations, early indications
suggest the European states will increasingly engage in European,
especially East Central European, ties, the Black Sea area nations
will activate their relations with Turkey and/or Iran, and the states
of Central Asia will seek their own ways in a world of Asian and
Islamic interests. It is important to note that all new states aspire to
become "normal" members of the international community and
that this desire provides the West with a lever—human rights—to
influence their behavior. Russia will likely be driven in different
directions: there will be calls to join Europe, pressure to enter into
close relations with Japan, and calls for striking a uniquely Russian
posture between East and West. The most pressing issues for
Russia will remain those formulated in the questions "what is
Russia? who is Russian?," and these will be answered at home.
Accordingly, the critical areas of concern for the world at large will
be the developments within Russia itself, followed by Russian-
Ukrainian relations and by the condition of Ukraine itself. It may
be easier to establish a democratic and stable government in Estonia or Latvia than in Russia or Ukraine, but the consequences of
a failure in the latter far exceed those in the former. Clearly, policies of nation building based on the community of citizenship
ought to receive encouragement and support. But it is also clear
that these are the most difficult policies to realize. A government
that is more expressly identified with the ethnic nation the state

takes its name from, but one which, nonetheless, grants the other nationalities broad cultural rights and admits them to political participation on equal terms clearly deserves more support than a government believing in ethnic supremacy.

No single solution is possible for the whole of the post-Soviet space. It is necessary to be prepared for a wide variety of solutions, some with precedents in the experience of other nations at other times, some quite novel and untried. But the general rule for the outside should be twofold: help avoid civil war; help build civil society. The course of economic reform and the progress of democracy will depend on how ethnic issues are resolved. The main conclusion of this survey is that in virtually all the states of the former Soviet Union the processes of state and nation building remain in the initial stage and that, accordingly, the "envelope of possibilities" still remains wide open. The prospects of very different outcomes are still great. This would suggest that external engagement in domestic and interrepublic affairs can have a significant impact on the processes discussed here and on their outcomes.

Notes

[1] Pipes (1968), pp. 296–297.
[2] Williams (1985), p. 338.
[3] Williams (1985), p. 338.
[4] Quoted in Szporluk (1981), p. 157
[5] Williams and Smith (1983), p. 502.
[6] Touraine (1988), pp. xix, 81–82.
[7] Lewis (1989).
[8] Szporluk (1989).
[9] Alexander Rutskoi, "V zashchitu Rossii," *Pravda,* January 30, 1992; and Alexander Rutskoi, "Prichastiye u Makdonal'dsa," *Izvestiya,* February 1, 1992.
[10] Solzhenitsyn (1991).
[11] Stanislav Kondrashov, "Novaia azbuka geografii, ili Pochemu nikak nel'zia bez Sodruzhestva," *Izvestiya,* January 15, 1992, p. 2.
[12] Williams (1985), p. 504.

4

The Military

STEPHEN M. MEYER

T hroughout the four-plus decades of the cold war the Soviet threat was captured in raw statistics of military power. Arrayed against the Western democracies were over 5 million uniformed personnel, some 27,000 nuclear weapons, 55,000 tanks, over 200 army divisions, 6,000 fighter/attack aircraft, 9,000 surface to air missile air defense launchers, almost 300 naval surface warships, and an equal number of attack submarines. This vast arsenal was deployed among thousands of missile sites, army and air bases, air defense posts, weapons depots, and naval facilities peppering the Soviet landscape.

STEPHEN M. MEYER is professor of defense and arms control studies and director of Soviet studies at the Massachusetts Institute of Technology. He serves as an advisor on Soviet security affairs to the Department of Defense, the State Department, the Office of Technology Assessment, and other government agencies. He has testified numerous times in open and closed hearings before the House Armed Services Committee, the Senate Armed Services Committee, the Senate Foreign Relations Committee, and the Senate Select Committee on Intelligence. Professor Meyer has published widely on Soviet national security affairs.

Armaments stocks were continuously modernized and aug-
mented by the labors of the gargantuan Soviet defense industrial
establishment. Over 500 defense research institutes and design
bureaus, twenty-four shipyards, and many thousands of arms
manufacturing enterprises were dispersed among the Soviet
republics. By the late 1980s Soviet defense industrial "floor space"
totaled roughly 600 million square feet—an increase of almost 60
percent since 1970.

For all intents and purposes the key numbers that seemed to so
aptly characterize Soviet military power remain unchanged today.
The size of existing weapons stocks and the enormous basing infrastructure have not declined appreciably. The number of defense
industrial facilities and the aggregate production floor space scattered among the post-Soviet states are virtually the same as before
the collapse of the Soviet Union.

The scale of these indicators notwithstanding, they belie the
true state of post-Soviet military power—as to some extent they
always did. To be sure, the post-Soviet strategic nuclear arsenal
remains fully capable of obliterating the United States and its
Western allies in a little less than an hour's time. But beyond this
doomsday scenario, post-Soviet military power is but a shadow of
its former self. In order to understand the current military capability and potential of the post-Soviet states one must examine the
two fundamental institutional legacies that remain in the wake of
the collapse of the Soviet Union: the military establishment and
the defense industrial establishment.

This chapter argues that today these two institutional pillars of
Soviet military power lie in shambles. Their institutional decay
renders meaningless the measures of military power to which we
have grown accustomed. Looking to the future, the institutional
survival of the former Soviet military establishment will depend on
its adoption by Russia and its transformation into the Russian
army—an event likely to materialize in the very near future.

In contrast, the former Soviet defense industrial establishment,
to the extent it can still be considered a viable and coherent institution, has virtually no hope of institutional survival. Its efforts at
self-preservation have actually hastened its disintegration.

The Soviet Military—
Managing Institutional Dismemberment

The Soviet military establishment, once a proud and professional organization that engendered fear and respect around the world, exists today as a disembodied specter. With the strange irony of having outlived its host state, the post-Soviet military continues to linger on as a fractured, directionless, demoralized, and politically disenfranchised institution. To the extent that this institution can still be considered a functioning "interest group," it is a supplicant lacking both patrons and convertible political capital. Meanwhile it has had to sacrifice organizational mission and professional development to an all-consuming chase to secure the basic necessities of daily life for its cadres. It is rapidly becoming an army barely capable of carrying out any major operation other than a suicidal nuclear war.

Institutional Health

Institutional health is a measure of the organization's ability to plan and behave as a functional organism. Is the organization's environment conducive to its operation? Does it have a clear sense of purpose and mission? Do its constituent parts operate coherently and in a coordinated manner? Is morale among the personnel strong and supportive of organizational activities? How well is it performing?

The Institutional Environment. The evaporation of the Soviet Union at the end of 1991 left the military establishment intact, but virtually destroyed its institutional environment. In particular there was no longer a well-defined political entity to which it could swear allegiance. Geophysically the "homeland" still existed, but politically it was splintering into over a dozen independent states—most of whom looked upon the former Soviet army as more of a threat than a defender.

The last minute cobbling together of the Commonwealth of Independent States did save the military establishment from instant dissolution, but there was never any real hope that it would become an authentic confederated political entity. From the outset many of the constituent states of the newly declared commonwealth, and most notably Ukraine, made it quite clear that the association was not to be considered the basis for defining a single "homeland" or "strategic space." Rather, it was merely a temporary forum for coordinating policies of independence and dividing up the spoils of the Soviet collapse—including military assets. In this framework the Soviet military—now the commonwealth military—was relegated to the role of caretaker of military facilities, hardware, and supplies until the new owners were ready to take possession.

None of the governments of the newly independent states evinces an intrinsic interest in the institutional welfare or development of the former Soviet military establishment. The broad base of influential patrons that used to support the military within the civilian political establishment is gone. They are replaced by significant adversaries among the new generation of post-Soviet politicians. At best, leaders such as Boris Yeltsin of Russia and Leonid Kravchuk of Ukraine pay lip service to the importance of the military as a symbol of state sovereignty. In Russia in particular there may also be some motivation to keep the military intact as a form of social welfare, that is to keep large numbers of young men off the unemployment and housing roles. But there are no real indications of substantive concern about military and military-institutional affairs. The post-Soviet states are in crisis, and they have far greater problems to worry about.

To make things worse antimilitary sentiments are strong in the post-Soviet societies at large. Politicians have more to gain by being antimilitary (or, at least indifferent) than by being promilitary. And societal attitudes even stifle existing laws and governmental attempts to provide some relief to the military establishment. For example, local food suppliers ignore republic government orders for goods to provision military garrisons, local governments refuse to assist in housing military personnel, and draftees simply ignore their call-up with the acquiescence of local governments. Understandably, the military establishment feels disenfranchised and abandoned.

Organizational Mission. Not only did the Soviet military lose its state identity, it also lost its raison d'être: the foreign threat. What loosely passes for post-Soviet military doctrine—a disjointed series of statements on military policy issued by commonwealth political leaders—has failed to answer any of the fundamental questions that are essential to defining the military's institutional mission. For what kind of war—nuclear or conventional, long or short, regional or global—should the armed forces of the commonwealth prepare? What besides war avoidance are the political goals of commonwealth military policy? And most importantly, who are the most likely potential foreign adversaries? No authoritative answers exist.

In fact not only are "threats" not acknowledged in the commonwealth's "military doctrine," they are specifically denied. Instead, political leaders anxious to break with the antagonistic Soviet past and gain access to Western economic aid have pronounced traditional "enemies" such as Germany and the United States to be friends. And so officials, businesspeople, and military officers of the "former threat" now scour former Soviet defense plants and bases examining equipment and technologies for sale and offering to finance the dismantling of the Soviet nuclear arsenal.

Cohesiveness and Morale. The evidence is indisputable that the post-Soviet military establishment is rent by fractures of every conceivable type and its officer corps plagued by desperation and hopelessness. Often portrayed solely in terms of ethnic strife, the splits within the post-Soviet military establishment are more diverse and complex.

To be sure, the divisive forces of nationalism that exploded in the Soviet Union during the latter half of the 1980s afflicted the military in a number of direct and indirect ways.[1] Most importantly, they created a clear breach between the officers (who were for the most part Russian and tended to identify strongly with the center) and the troops (who were not Russian in the majority and increasingly identified with their home republic). It also reinforced divisive tendencies among the troops as ethnic gangs formed to protect their own and to harass others. Violence occurred in many units, destroying cohesion, discipline, and readiness.

In the post-Soviet world the divisive effects of national identity have worked their way into the officer corps as well. The commonwealth has not been a powerful magnet for officer loyalties. The republics—most notably Ukraine—directly assaulted military institutional loyalties by requiring oaths of allegiance to the republic government. Such endeavors have been made more appealing by the fact that with each passing month it is the individual republic governments, not the commonwealth, that are paying and provisioning the armed forces on their territory. Institutional loyalties are being supplanted by what might be termed "provisioning" loyalties. Officers are shifting their allegiance to governments that pay them and provide food and housing. Disturbingly, in some isolated instances military units even seem to be affiliating with local governments.

Interservice rivalries have also intensified in the wake of severe budget and personnel cuts. All current and impending military reform and reorganization efforts incorporate major amalgamations of forces with some services swallowing up parts of others. Thus the scramble is on as each branch of the armed forces attempts to preserve what is left of its own identity and resources. Here military institutional loyalties are being supplanted by service loyalties.

It is doubtful that morale among the officer corps—which in essence defines a military establishment—could be lower. Living and working conditions are abysmal. Even with the series of raises recently offered, military wages lag behind to the point that many officers and their families live below the official poverty level. Most officers are pulling double duty to compensate for the severe understaffing in the units. The amount of effort expended on provisioning their troops and doing double duty has eroded officer self-image. Consequently, the youngest and most talented officers are leaving service to accept well paying jobs in cooperatives.

The fateful attempts to use the armed forces to suppress domestic disturbances had extremely corrosive effects on institutional discipline and self-image. Beginning with attempts to use military units to put down disturbances in Tbilisi in 1989, followed by Baku in 1990, Vilnius in 1991, and ending with the failed coup of August 1991, the military establishment learned that institutional cohesion, discipline, and political fortune always suffered in the aftermath of such activities.

As a result a "Tbilisi syndrome" quickly beset the military. Commanders realized that they would always be better off refusing orders to intervene in public disturbances. This psychology was strongly reinforced by events following the August 1991 coup. Commanders who avoided by whatever means following orders to impose martial law remain in command; those who did as their superiors ordered were dismissed. The lesson was clear: when in doubt, do nothing.

This attitude has eroded the very heart of military command and discipline by creating pervasive uncertainty regarding what constitutes legitimate orders from civilian and military superiors. The military establishment is now a consensual organization, where officers and units take direction from above on a case-by-case basis. They vote on whether to follow orders.

Lastly, military professionalism has been devastated. Ironically, all of the efforts toward military reform over the past several years were intended to increase professionalism. The military was shedding its responsibilities in construction, transportation, policing, harvesting, and menial labor. But the reverse has occurred. As is described below, the military has had to abandon professional pursuits for simple survival. In essence, today the post-Soviet military establishment exists to exist.

Performance Capabilities. The political, social, and economic turmoil that began several years ago and continues to engulf the post-Soviet states today has eroded military combat readiness to an unimaginable degree. The effects are manifest in the two principal components of military power: personnel and equipment.

Large numbers of conscripts, which still make up the great mass of the troops, continue to ignore draft orders. A growing number of soldiers are deserting their units, unnerved by their postings outside their home republics. Many of the most talented junior officers continue to resign to seek employment in the cooperative sector. As a result, many supposedly "100 percent ready" units are missing more than half of their personnel—including key commanders. In a number of units conscripts have been used to replace missing lieutenants and captains as commanders.

Meanwhile the general provisioning of forces in the field has collapsed. Units have not received authorized supplies of food, clothing, and fuel. Not only does this affect the immediate physical and psychological abilities of the troops, but it quickly leads to the abandonment of military training. Instead units set out in search of work opportunities to provision themselves, and detachments fan out over the countryside trying to locate food and goods for purchase. There have even been reported instances of Strategic Rocket Troops (units operating mobile ICBMs) threatening to end field deployment and return to their main operating base unless field provisions were made available.

As has been well reported in the Western press, hundreds of thousands of officers and their families continue to live without adequate housing, bivouacked in tents or emptied military vehicles. (The military housing shortage has also had serious international repercussions: commonwealth military units still in Germany and the Baltic states have refused to return home until housing is guaranteed.) Building materials are scarce, and when available extremely expensive. For those lucky enough to have housing, fuel is frequently unavailable from central military stocks for heating and cooking. Units do not have sufficient financial resources to purchase supplies from local markets.

In an attempt to alleviate the support problem, the Ministry of Defense decreed that beginning in 1992 officers, units, and other military organizations could sell their services to civilians to raise money. Tank repair crews are now free to hire themselves out as auto mechanics. Infantry companies can work as paid day laborers in the fields and factories. Security details can seek employment as private security guards. Naval officers, one assumes, can book sailing tours. Surplus equipment can be sold off.

Naturally, such entrepreneurial endeavors are only supposed to occur on personal leave time. In reality they are occurring full time. Thus, even in units with adequate provisions, traditional professional military pursuits are being abandoned in favor of earning additional revenue by outside contracting. It is hard to imagine how the military establishment can expect to maintain its institutional identity, let alone any type of esprit de corps, when it transforms itself into a temporary service business.

The decline in equipment readiness is equally bad. First, as mentioned above, a military-technical "brain drain" has been underway for several years. Skilled officers and technical support personnel have left the military. Their replacements are far less qualified to handle the complex equipment. Thus, equipment breakdown rates are accelerating as repair rates are declining.

Meanwhile the supply of spare parts and service material needed to keep military hardware operational has all but dried up. One illustrative case involves the single plant that produced a special oil required by 40 percent of all military aircraft engines. The plant's management decided to stop producing the oil so it could switch to more profitable products. When reserve stocks are exhausted a significant portion of the former Soviet air force will be grounded. Similarly, few tanks are used in field training exercises these days, due to the shortage of oil pumps and filters, as well as fuel. Cannibalization has become commonplace in order to keep some number of weapons operational.

Correspondingly, field training has been cut back in order to conserve dwindling supplies and to minimize wear and tear on the equipment that remains operational.

Even new equipment is arriving in the field missing crucial components, with no hope that those parts will ever be supplied. Weapons systems are being deployed with operational units despite the fact that they are not yet in operational condition. The Tu-160 BLACKJACK strategic bomber is one prominent example of a weapon "in service" that actually spends most of its time grounded due to inoperative systems.

The bottom line is clear. With the exception of the Strategic Forces none of the commonwealth's other services is in any condition to mount a major military operation. The Strategic Forces are an exception because of the peculiar nature of their mission, not because they have received special access to supplies.

Coping Strategies

The military establishment's primary objective has been first and foremost to maintain the institutional integrity of the armed forces and the central command. Preserving operational capabilities is important as well, but has taken a back seat to ensuring institutional survival. When the August 1991 coup d'état presented the military with the trade-off of preserving the old system by supporting the coup, but with the very strong likelihood that the military itself would fracture, it chose to back away. Institutional preservation took precedence.

Allegiance Shifting. The military's coping strategy can be summarized by this phrase: shift allegiance to whatever political authority seems most capable of keeping the institution intact. During the last two years of the Soviet Union, when the Communist party was rapidly losing its authority, the Soviet military shifted its institutional subordination to the Soviet state. It followed Gorbachev's shift in power from the party to the state. The Soviet presidency became the locus for military subordination.

In the wake of the August 1991 coup, political power drained rapidly from the center to the republics. The Russian government in particular was taking control of all the key levers of political, economic, and diplomatic administration. By the late fall it became obvious that the only way to save the military establishment was to gingerly shift institutional allegiance to the Yeltsin government. There was never any chance that the Soviet military would remain with Gorbachev; he had already surrendered state fiscal and budgetary powers to Yeltsin.

When the Soviet Union dissolved and the commonwealth was born the Soviet military became the Armed Forces of the Commonwealth of Independent States, and it was subordinated to the Council of Heads of State of the Commonwealth. But that body never matured into a truly functional executive, nor has it ever spoken with a unified voice, as did the old Defense Council/Politburo of the Soviet Union. As former Chief of the General Staff General Vladimir Lobov lamented, no one in the military knows

who speaks with authority for the civilian leadership on commonwealth military matters.

By default the commonwealth armed forces had no institutional
alternative but to recognize the implicit head of the commonwealth, Russian president Boris Yeltsin, as the supreme civil authority. (The commonwealth leaders did vest Yeltsin with control
over the nuclear forces.) The truth is that most of the middle and
senior officer corps and most certainly those in the central apparatus of the Ministry of Defense and General Staff identify with
Russia as the de facto heir to Soviet military power. Thus it is easy
and comfortable to look to the Russian president as the seat of civil
authority under the facade of subordination to the commonwealth.

Warlordism. When one moves down the chain of command
into the field, however, the situation becomes a bit cloudier. As
already noted, for a host of political, economic, and professional
reasons there are divided loyalties among the lower ranks. Political
and economic chaos coupled with institutional decay have left
many field units to fend for themselves. When the central military
establishment is unable to properly provision and support field
units and local governments move in to offer superior assistance,
then unit survival strategies mimic those of the parent institution.
That is, they move to shift allegiance. While most commanders
and units still look to Moscow, some have placed themselves at the
disposal of Minsk, Kiev, and even rebellious provinces that are
able to provide financing, food, and shelter.[2]

Military Coups. At this point one has to raise the seemingly
obvious question: why isn't a military coup d'état a viable coping
strategy? Why doesn't a disenfranchised, impoverished, and dis-
gruntled military seize power? But Bonapartism or equivalent
Latin American or African models do not apply. Strong institutional, professional, and practical considerations leave the military
establishment neither inclined nor capable of taking control of
Russia, let alone the commonwealth.

First and foremost the institutional decay described earlier
makes the military incapable of functioning so decisively—no con-

sensus for a political takeover is possible. Second, the crosscutting institutional problems that plague the military establishment cannot be remedied by seizing political control. Indeed, they would be greatly exacerbated. This was widely perceived among the officer corps during the August 1991 coup, and validated in its aftermath.

Third, the chaotic political and economic environment among the post-Soviet states means that there is little of administrative or substantive utility to seize. The old economic and political command structures are gone and cannot be restored. Fourth, existing antimilitary sentiments in society would be further inflamed by the presumption that the military would take care of itself first. Military units would be required to maintain civil control with the frightening possibility that what remaining institutional discipline exists would evaporate. A coup would ensure the institutional disintegration of the military.

The ambivalence of the situation is revealed by a poll among Russian officers taken in March 1992. It showed that only 17 percent approved of Yeltin's reforms. Some 56 percent opposed them. But a full 90 percent believed that the governing of Russia should be left to politicians.

This does not mean that some fragment of the military could not act precipitously in support of a coup by nationalist political figures, as happened in the August 1991 coup. It is almost certain, however, that other fragments of the military would actively side with legitimate authorities in opposing such a move, while still other elements of the military would sit on the sidelines and watch.

Nor can one dismiss the possibility of "warlordism"—the formation of political-military mafias—as a coping strategy at local levels. The state governments of Russia, Ukraine, and the other republics do not exert control over much of their territories. Most locales are on their own. Thus the covert or overt takeover of local politics by a military commander cannot be ruled out.

Military Reform. Military reform has been used for several years as a coping strategy to preserve both institutional integrity and operational capabilities in an uncertain environment. In an attempt to preempt civilian efforts to intrude onto its professional turf, the military promulgated its own "new ideas" for command structures, organization, strategy, and personnel policy that reflected its preference for incremental and piecemeal change. The details need not be discussed, since events have rendered this strategy meaningless. It is noteworthy, however, that the military was willing to consider even more radical changes as the threats to its institutional survival increased.

Implications for the Post-Soviet Militaries

Ironically the only cure for the institutional ills plaguing the post-Soviet military establishment lies in its dismemberment and division among the post-Soviet states. The facade of a stateless commonwealth armed forces must end. It may seem counterintuitive to believe that an institution can be saved by breaking it up, but the logic becomes clear when it is realized that the post-Soviet military establishment cannot have an organizational mission or an institutional identity, nor can it return to the path of professionalization, until it regains a state based identity. Institutional definition and cohesion require that the command, control, and support of the armed forces be a routine part of state based governmental administration. Otherwise, institutional collapse and "warlordism" will follow.

From an institutional perspective, carving up the former Soviet military establishment is made more palatable by the fact that Russia will inherit the bulk of it. More than half of former Soviet military bases are located on Russian soil, a number that grossly underestimates the actual proportion of forces that are based there. Russia is, moreover, footing at least 80 percent of the bill for the present commonwealth armed forces. The Ministry of Defense/General Staff apparat has always been composed of at least 90 percent Russian nationals. Thus when the parsing is complete, much of former Soviet military establishment will at last find a political home as the Russian armed forces.

National Armies. It is a curious fact that the Russian political leadership has moved much more hesitantly than the other republic leaderships in forming its own army. The reasons are fundamentally political, not military. First, the Russian leadership understood full well that the commonwealth armed forces were, for all intents and purposes, the Russian armed forces. Second, many of the other former Soviet republics harbored latent fears about resurgent Russian imperialism. Avoiding the formal declaration of a Russian army, and seeming to bind the former Soviet military in a commonwealth framework, represented good interrepublic politics. Third, the exercise of joint military planning and coordination under the commonwealth banner gave the Russian leadership some entree into military policy making in the other republics. Indeed, the Russian government has used the implicit threat of declaring its own armed forces to slow the march toward formally establishing national armed forces in Ukraine and elsewhere.

Nevertheless the facade of the commonwealth banner cannot last too much longer. As Ukraine and Belarus proceed to firmly establish the basis for their own armed forces and render meaningless the commonwealth banner, Russia will follow suit. The nominal creation of a Russian Ministry of Defense in March 1992 was just the first step. The question, then, is what type of military establishments will emerge? First and foremost, we should be careful not to confuse the military windfalls that the post-Soviet states will inherit with sustainable and enduring military postures. Beyond the first few years the post-Soviet militaries will not bear much resemblance to their initial form. In particular, with the exception of Russia, most of what they will acquire from the former Soviet largess will be beyond their indigenous capacities to use and maintain. Thus the force structures and postures that emerge over the next year from this writing will be heavily inflated and bizarrely skewed in appearance; the longer run military postures of all the post-Soviet states will be significantly smaller and less capable.

Second, none of the post-Soviet governments including Russia has the slightest idea of military needs or even how to go about determining what they might be. No "threats and requirements based" defense planning is underway. Instead the definition of post-Soviet national military forces is being driven by the basic political notion that all sovereign states must have their own armed forces. Consequently a strange combination of inheritance, economic and social policy, symbolism, and elementary heuristics will initially shape the regional post-Soviet military balance.

Russia, for example, will take possession of the armed forces of the commonwealth in roughly intact condition—except for the ground forces. Inheriting the old Soviet Ministry of Defense command and its General Staff, Russia will become the repository of Soviet military thought, military science, and military traditions. This is a critical aspect of institutional survival for the former Soviet military. (It also raises the risk that the new Russian Ministry of Defense will be more concerned with preserving its former institutional structure and pattern than in devising new, more appropriate ones.)

Looking at the armed services, the Russian Strategic Deterrent Forces will eventually gather all the strategic nuclear weapons of the former Soviet Union under one roof.[3] Economic, social, and political pressures will push the force significantly below the START warhead ceiling.

As a result of a recent reorganization, this service will also control early warning functions and national air defense—including ballistic missile defense represented by the Moscow ABM system. The Russian ground forces, air forces, and navy will continue as independent services, ultimately with much smaller numbers of personnel and equipment. The Russian air forces and navy will walk away with the vast majority of weaponry they controlled under Soviet auspices, but the Russian ground forces will lose control over a considerable stock of conventional land arms. The reason is simple: the other republics have the nominal potential to operate and maintain many of the latter.

Over the course of the decade, the overall size of the Russian armed forces may shrink below 1.5 million troops, though initially the number could remain substantially larger. This delay in demobilizing will be the consequence of economic-social concerns, not military requirements. With the Russian economy still in free-fall and tremors of social unrest just below the surface, it would be a dangerous gamble to suddenly release many hundreds of thousands if not millions of unemployed and homeless young men. Maintaining a Russian draft will help to check unemployment among the young. Retaining a large officer corps will not exacerbate the housing crunch. Basically, maintaining a "bloated" military establishment for several more years might be a wise form of social welfare and social control.

It is likely that Russia will enter into military pacts with a number of the Central Asian republics, where commonwealth forces are presently deployed. Many of these have neither the inclination nor the resources to build their own armies. Such NATO-type pacts would offer basing rights for Russian forces.

Ukraine will undoubtedly build its own armed forces. The same seems true for Belarus, though on a much smaller scale. Neither state, however, has offered a threat-and-requirements analysis to back its desire for a military establishment. Instead, it is quite clear that their rush to build a national armed forces is a demonstration of national political sovereignty. It is in this context that one should also interpret the ongoing disputes between Russia and Ukraine regarding the disposition of nuclear weapons, the Black Sea Fleet, and the remaining spoils of the Red Army. These disagreements have almost nothing to do with issues of military balance. They are political contests over sovereignty and liquidation rights.

Thus when queried about their likely military postures, both Ukrainian and Belarusian authorities explain that among "normal states" armed forces personnel usually represents 0.6 to 0.8 percent of their populations. This logic implies that Ukraine should have about 450,000 troops under arms, and Belarus about 80,000. They also point out that "normal states" spend about 4 percent of their GNPs on their militaries.

The simplicity and elegance of such senseless calculations notwithstanding, the Ukrainian and Belarusian armed forces will probably tally in at one-half to one-quarter of these numbers. Economic and industrial realities will constrain political impulses. The ground forces will dominate both military establishments. A small Ukrainian air force is conceivable, but not without Russian—or foreign—willingness to provide spare parts. It is doubtful, however, that Ukraine will have the resources to purchase Western military aircraft or parts in quantity.

A small Ukrainian flotilla is also a possibility, but it will be largely a symbolic force. Ukraine will not have the fuels or oils required to maintain a large fleet. In this context, its dispute with

Russia over the disposition of the Black Sea Fleet is political-eco-
nomic in nature, not military. It must be understood in terms of
asserting national sovereignty and who gets the liquidation rights
to sell the ships on the world market—and not who gets to have a
national navy.

Certainly other post-Soviet states will absorb the largess left
behind by the former Soviet military. Armenia, Azerbaijan, and
Georgia have already proven the utility of this approach. These
forces will be only of local significance, appropriate for carrying
out internecine warfare and civil war.

Militias. There has been considerable confusion in the West
regarding the formation of National Guard (militia) units and armies in the post-Soviet states. The former are quite distinct from
standing armed forces. Drawing on former internal troops (MVD)
and KGB troops to fill the ranks, the national militias will be
intended primarily for regime protection, natural disaster relief,
and other forms of "domestic use." The need for national militias
for regime protection was one of the main lessons of the August
1991 coup.

In countries such as Russia and Ukraine militias will exist in
parallel with national armed forces. The Russian National Guard
will most likely be of the order of 50,000 to 100,000 troops. Ukrainian authorities are talking in terms of 30,000 to 50,000 troops.
Belarus is contemplating 10,000. In other states, such as Kazakhstan, they may exist in lieu of armed forces, and number in the low
thousands.

The Atomization of Defense Industries

The other great institution of Soviet military power—the defense industrial establishment—has shattered. While its research
and development (R&D) and production facilities remain intact
and many continue to produce goods, the controlling mechanisms
and structures that made the Soviet defense industrial establishment a coherent and functioning organism have been destroyed.
The Military Industrial Commission (VPK), the State Planning
Agency (GOSPLAN), the State Supply Agency (GOSNAB), and

the Communist party no longer exist; chaos has taken their place. Without the planning, prioritizing, directing, allocating, and coordinating activities of these higher level organizations, scores of individual defense enterprises are shutting down haphazardly, snapping the taut supply chain that made the Soviet defense industrial sector work.

As is discussed below, the self-preservation strategies adopted by the defense industries have only served to exacerbate the institutional disintegration of the defense industrial establishment. They have resulted in the atomization and general technological regression of the defense industrial base.

Institutional Health

The Institutional Environment of the Good Old Days. In order to understand what is happening to the post-Soviet defense industrial establishment and why the prognosis for its future is so grim, one has to first understand how things were in "the good old days." The Soviet defense industries evolved in a political and economic environment that was uniquely protective and nurturing. For most of the history of the Soviet Union the country's leaders subscribed to the belief that Soviet economic development was synonymous with defense industrial development. The "military-industrial complex" never had to pressure Soviet leaders to finance and supply it—Soviet leaders identified with it.

Communist party departments and governmental organizations and agencies at all levels were set up to facilitate defense industrial growth. The Military Industrial Commission (VPK) was created to set defense industrial priorities, to plan and coordinate the work of all the defense industrial ministries, and to ensure that the other government ministries responded rapidly to defense sector needs. The State Planning Agency and the State Supply Agency devised their annual and five-year plans to ensure that the defense production system was not disrupted by supply interruptions. Supply problems did nevertheless arise, and when they did the Communist party stepped in with a heavy hand to squeeze the needed goods out of the economy.

Defense enterprises received near absolute priority on materials, labor, and investment funding. Sudden demands for materials and supplies by defense industries were met by reducing further allocations to civilian industry. Defense enterprises were able to "borrow" money from state banks, often with no interest, and ultimately without the requirement to pay back the principal.

Most of the Soviet defense industrial base was vertically integrated with single suppliers for most commodities. Largely for political and social-economic reasons, supply networks for every individual weapons system stretched out across the territory of the entire Soviet Union. Thus to build a tank in Kiev hundreds of components had to be shipped in from monopoly suppliers located in the Baltics, Russia, and Central Asia. The VPK, GOSPLAN, GOSNAB, and ultimately the Communist party made sure the system worked.

By the 1980s maintaining high levels of defense sector output had become such a political obsession that defense industries were producing weapons in quantities that frequently exceeded military orders and with qualities significantly below military requirements. Serial production of armaments became both a means and an end in itself. Defense policy seemed to be the servant of defense industrial policy. Illustrations abound. So many superfluous ICBMs were delivered to the Strategic Rocket Forces in the 1970s and 1980s that they eventually were just stacked in warehouses. Of the dozens of the Tu-160 BLACKJACK strategic bombers delivered to the air force from 1984–91 none is in operational condition. Ministry of Aviation field teams are permanently housed at flight bases to try to make the aircraft usable. Every unit of a new model tactical engagement radar delivered to the navy over the past several years has been completely inoperable and unrepaired since delivery. Yet the defense industries continued to receive wages, bonuses, incentive funds, and the like.

The Institutional Environment of Today. That nurturing environment no longer exists. A chaotic and basically hostile environment has replaced it. In retrospect, it is not clear that Gorbachev's economic reforms of the late 1980s set the stage. First there were the self-financing and cost-accounting reforms. Defense enterprises were expected to cover their operating costs without heavy government subsidization. Though subsidies were never actually reduced, enterprise planning, budgeting, and operations were nonetheless thrown into turmoil in anticipation of the change in policy. Prices for defense goods started to rise while production bottlenecks proliferated.

Next came freezes, then reductions, and finally the wholesale elimination of major weapons procurement programs. Defense industrial production started to unravel. For example, in 1986 a fissile material production facility in Kazakhstan was instructed to prepare to double output in the 1990s. Capital investment was channeled accordingly. Then in 1990 it received orders to cut current production by 75 percent. The sudden cancellation of orders in the aviation, shipbuilding, and missile industries—a harbinger of what was to come—sent many enterprises into panic.

By the last half of 1991 most enterprises had lost between 40 and 90 percent of their defense orders. R&D projects suffered equally decimating cuts. This was in part a consequence of mandated cuts in defense R&D and procurement funding, but it was also a result of runaway inflation in the defense sector. The two proved to be a deadly combination. For example, the commonwealth air force estimates that procurement funding for aircraft was cut 50 percent between 1988 and 1991, while prices rose simultaneously four times. In other words, military aircraft funding in 1991 was sufficient to purchase a little over 12 percent of what was procured in 1987.

Today defense orders barely trickle down. Most plants run at a small fraction of their capacity. Priority access to human, material, and financial resources has ended. There are no government agencies or political organizations dedicated to preserving and supporting the defense sector. If anything it is viewed as a cash cow by government officials and many overly entrepreneurial defense industrialists.

Organizational Mission. The fundamental organizational mission of the military industrial establishment—armaments production—came under assault with the ill-fated effort at planned defense conversion. In 1987 and 1988 the Gorbachev regime, fear-ing social upheaval, ordered the defense industries to take on added responsibilities for civilian manufacturing. The defense sector had always produced civilian goods as a sideline, but now priorities were to be reversed.

The Ministry of Light Industry was abolished, and its plants were assigned to the defense industrial ministries. Defense R&D and production enterprises were ordered by the Central Committee of the Communist party to assist in the development and production of agroindustrial machinery, food processing equipment, household goods, food servicing (restaurant equipment), and medical and rehabilitation equipment.

This peculiar assignment was resisted and resented by the defense industrial establishment. The equal priority assigned to defense production and conversion production manifested itself by a noticeable decline in the former and a negligible increase in the latter. The defense sector was losing profits, skilled labor was quitting to join private cooperatives, and the prognosis for future defense production was getting worse.

By the end of 1988 the VPK realized that if the institutional identity and mission of the defense industrial sector was going to be preserved it would have to gain control of the conversion agenda. In 1989 it presented its own conversion plan to Gorbachev. Emphasizing "dual-use" technologies, priority would be given to microelectronics, computers, information technologies, communications, transport infrastructure, civil aviation, civil space, and materials. The VPK hoped to use conversion to spark a new infusion of capital into the defense industrial base and to retool defense plants with dual-use technologies.

The VPK plan sat on Gorbachev's desk until mid-1991, when there were indications that the regime, recognizing the failure of earlier conversion attempts, was planning to adopt the VPK strategy. Had the August 1991 coup succeeded, it is likely that this plan would have become the foundation of Soviet economic policy. The coup's failure, however, marked the end of coordinated institutional efforts at self-preservation.

Cohesiveness and Morale. Following the failure of the August 1991 coup, the central planning and administrative organiza-

tions of the defense industrial establishment—the VPK, GOS-
PLAN, GOSNAB, and the defense industrial ministries—were
abolished. The Communist party, the political bastion of defense
industrial interests in the Soviet state, was outlawed. Without these
organizations, the defense industrial establishment was no longer
able to function as a coherent, mission oriented institution. The
coffin was nailed shut when the Soviet Union itself dissolved, and
the political geography of the defense industries broke up among
fifteen independent states.

With the institutional structure gone, defense enterprises were
on their own. Since the beginning of 1992 every defense industrial
facility has teetered on the brink of collapse. It is difficult to characterize the depths to which managerial and worker morale have
sunk. There is no basis for thinking things will improve, and ample
reason to expect them to get worse. In essence, defense production
is no longer the priority of any of the post-Soviet states, and the
shambles of the post-Soviet economy makes it unlikely that anything could be accomplished even if it were.

Performance Capabilities. The severing of the "firm hand"
of the central planning system has not yet been replaced by the
"invisible hand" of the free market. Some defense orders continue
to move through the system. But pricing and payment are haphaz-
ard at best. Many plants have not been paid for goods that have
been ordered. The rapid succession of procurement budget cuts in
1991–92 left many defense producers holding onto expensive
goods in the wake of cancelled orders. As a result, many component suppliers are refusing future defense orders.

In other cases, lacking administrative guidance or market cues,
defense plants are operating on autopilot. Defense goods continue
to be produced—albeit in far smaller quantities and often lacking
in essential components—despite an absence of orders. Organizational inertia keeps them going. Some producers continue to receive input materials and components from former suppliers. Others are using components and materials previously stockpiled as a
hedge against supply interruption.[4]

This cannot, however, continue for long. The defense supply
structure is collapsing in on itself, and reserve stocks of supplies are

being exhausted. Individual defense enterprises all across the former Soviet Union are taking themselves off-line and ceasing manufacture of vital parts, components, and supplies for which they had been the sole supplier for years, if not decades. Some cannot get the needed input components themselves. Others have found nondefense customers willing to pay more for their product, or they are switching to more profitable products.

Other plants are shutting down entirely, as in the case of the only plant in the former Soviet Union that manufactured parachutes for military personnel. It seems that its sole supplier of parachute-grade silk simply cut off supplies without warning. The silk suppliers found that far greater profits could be made selling their product to clothing cooperatives. When no other silk source could be found the parachute plant closed.

Meanwhile the defense industries are experiencing a brain drain. The most talented engineers, skilled workers, and managers are moving out to form private corporations and businesses. As is described below, they often take with them substantial capital and material assets. As a result the overall technological and productive capability of defense industries is declining.

Coping Strategies

With the superstructure of the defense industrial establishment in ruins, the organizational imperative of self-preservation has pushed defense enterprises to pursue individual survival strategies. This is the equivalent of industrial "warlordism." At least five distinct strategies are discernible: (1) degenerate conversion, (2) mortgaging, (3) seeking foreign investment, (4) contracting for foreign arms sales, and (5) localizing supply and production. All are aimed at individual enterprise survival, rather than institutional survival, and all are hastening the "atomization" of the defense industries.

Degenerate Conversion. The conversion that is taking place among the post-Soviet defense industries today bears no resemblance to the planned, systematic, coordinated, and economically responsive conversion programs that captured the imagination of

Soviet politicians and industrial bureaucrats. Instead laboratory
directors and plant managers are engaged in frantic, unguided,
uninformed, chaotic, and highly idiosyncratic searches for one or
more civilian products to replace lost military orders. Finally convinced that the good old days are gone, they are looking for anything to keep their doors open and their workers employed. There
is no attempt to coordinate production changes with other defense
plants. This is *degenerate conversion.*

In almost all cases degenerate conversion results in sophisticated
defense production being replaced by more labor-intensive, lower
technology production. As was noted above, this is precisely what
defense industrialists railed against in the late 1980s and what the
VPK was trying to prevent with its conversion scheme: regressive
industrialization. The Irkutsk Aircraft Production Association, for
example, was once a production and repair center for highly sophisticated military jet aircraft. Today its primary "conversion"
products include children's toys, aluminum dishes, washboards,
choppers, back packs, and tents. Degenerate conversion is likely to
define the future of most surviving defense plants. While it may
serve immediate plant needs and even fill local consumer demand,
it is not a likely engine for near-term national economic recovery.

Mortgaging. How do enterprises continue to fund themselves
in this chaotic environment? The lucky ones receive partial and
temporary wage subsidies from their republic governments. Most
have been mortgaging their futures in a desperate effort to stay
alive, hoping that "the good times" will return.

In order to retain their skilled labor force, many defense enterprises are using "banked" capital investment and maintenance
funds to pay wages. Allocated during the last years of the Gorbachev regime and intended to finance plant retooling, technological
modernization, and new construction, these funds were socked
away by enterprise managers. Using them to pay wages will make
it impossible for most enterprises to convert to all but the simplest
civilian products, let alone upgrade production technology.

Similarly, social incentive funds—money held by defense enterprises to build schools, hospitals, and housing—are also being used
to pay wages. On the one hand, this helps to retain skilled labor

and management. On the other hand, as the perks and living conditions decline, because social incentive funds are being diverted, skilled workers are still leaving.

Other defense employers have turned to the nascent commercial loan market to cover plant wages. Much to their surprise they are expected to pay back both principal and double-digit interest to the new banks. A number of major weapons producers have taken on huge debt loads, each totaling hundreds of millions of rubles, in order to continue financing operations. Most will go bankrupt unless state governments bail them out.

Foreign Investment. A third strategy involves the pursuit of foreign investment. Prior to the breakup of the Soviet Union the VPK had attempted to stimulate foreign investment. It was a bold effort to use Western capital and technology to revitalize the Soviet defense base.

With the demise of the defense sector's central organs, efforts to lure foreign investors have become decentralized and uncoordinated, falling to enterprise managers and local officials. Again the emphasis is on obtaining Western aid to keep plants operating, for refurbishing the defense industrial plant technology base, retaining skilled workers, and ultimately gaining access to Western markets.[5] Not surprisingly the new post-Soviet entrepreneurs tend to greatly overstate their indigenous capabilities. Potential foreign investors are being exposed to a wide variety of industrial Potemkin villages.

The combination of degenerate conversion and the effort to attract foreign investment has, in turn, led to *industrial parasitism.* Management at an increasing number of key defense industrial enterprises is forming private "associations" (corporations) to help them attract foreign capital and sell their goods abroad. These associations skim the cream off their parent defense enterprises— siphoning off the best management, the high-technology assets, capital, and the top 5–10 percent of the enterprise's skilled labor force. When possible they sell off fixed assets they do not want, but that they also do not own. The great bulk of the enterprise is left to rot. A good illustration is the Leningrad Optical Association, one of the few Soviet defense industries to attract serious attention by

Western investors. The actual defense enterprise is reported to employ almost 25,000 workers. But less than 900 are part of the new association. If this becomes the model for post-Soviet defense conversion, 95 out of every 100 defense workers will be unemployed.

Foreign Arms Sales. A fourth putative strategy is not to convert at all, but rather to sell arms overseas. Increasingly, this option is attracting the attention of both political leaders and industrial managers in the post-Soviet states. It certainly makes sense from the defense industrialists point of view, because it allows defense enterprises to do what they have always done best. Even better, they can earn hard currency at world prices. There is, of course, a large installed Soviet arms client base around the world. Presumably, they represent a market for spare parts and modernized weaponry.

Localization. Localization involves the formation of islands of financial-industrial autonomy at the city or regional level. It represents a complete departure of the former Soviet system where vertically integrated supply networks reached across the entire length of the country. The hope is that local employment can be stabilized, thereby stabilizing local politics. If this model works, a kind of feudalistic economy would eventually evolve.

In its present incarnation localization connotes the formation of local "mafias," bringing together local defense industrialists; former Communist party, VPK, and KGB officials (who hold a surprising amount of investment capital); bankers; politicians; and even military officers. It is not surprising that the former Communist party, KGB, and VPK officials form the core of the financing and commodity exchanges. The latter in particular are essential for locating vital input supplies.

Implications for the Post-Soviet Economies

It is reasonable to assume that the redirection and resuscitation of the defense industries could "save" local economies. Pockets of autonomous industrial growth could appear on the post-Soviet

landscape. However, these will be basic industries, not high technology. To a large extent they will be isolated and highly vulnerable.

In particular, localization combined with degenerate conversion and foreign arms sales may succeed in preserving individual
and regional industrial capabilities, and even basic defense industrial production—small arms, ammunition, artillery systems, military vehicles, and the like. Theoretically, over time local industrial
concerns could link up with other such groups, and establish the
foundation for a regional economy.

This may be the best long-term hope for the post-Soviet economies, especially in the small states. It would mean rebuilding their
economies from the ground up. For the larger republics, however,
the time scale is probably of the order of a decade and more before
a national industrial system will emerge. Nonetheless, the transformation of the old defense industrial base cannot serve as the engine for rapid national economic revitalization among the post-
Soviet states. It is not, nor was it ever, the magic reservoir of
resources, talent, or special capabilities that many believed.

What about the prospects for weapons production among the
post-Soviet states? With the exception of Russia, the defense industries left behind by the collapse of the Soviet Union will not be
up to the task of undertaking a major rearming or modernization
of the post-Soviet military establishments. The remnants of the old
Soviet defense industrial system with its broad dispersal of component suppliers and the monopoly supply structure left no republic,
save Russia, with the complete manufacturing and supply base to
produce major weaponry. Thus the fact that the final assembly
plant for SS-18 ICBMs is located in Ukraine is interesting, but not
terribly important, since most of the components are made elsewhere.

In fact more than 70 percent of the former Soviet Union's defense industrial base remains in Russia. It is well known that
Ukraine holds the second largest share at about 15 percent. That
comprises about 1 million defense workers. While that may seem
large, some perspective is gained when one considers that that is
the same number of defense workers employed in St. Petersburg
alone.

Therefore the military establishments of the post-Soviet states—again with the exception of Russia—will most likely have to be content for many years to come with their depreciating Soviet "inheritance" plus the small arms, rifles, mortars, simple artillery, and basic vehicles that their countries may be capable of producing and maintaining. To be sure, such weapons will be sufficient for interrepublic warfare and arms trade to weak states, but they will not figure prominently in deciding regional military balances. In order to acquire anything more substantial the post-Soviet states will have to barter their goods for arms from Russia.

This also suggests that while defense industrialists may continue to be a major force in local politics within the post-Soviet states, they are unlikely to regain the influence and prominence they had in the Soviet era. Former Communist party bureaucrats and VPK and KGB officials, however, may regain national clout by virtue of their growing stranglehold on financial and commodity resources.

Implications for International Security

Everyone in the West cheers the dismantling of Soviet military power. As we watch the post-Soviet states struggle to assemble their polities and economies, however, one cannot help but wonder about the dark cloud that invariably accompanies the silver lining.

Reversibility

The most obvious concern is "reversibility." Could a strong and aggressive military power rise from the ashes of the former Soviet Union? This chapter argues that only Russia can conceivably pose that threat, and then only over the long term. Putting aside suicidal nuclear scenarios, Russia today can only muster the conventional capability to threaten other post-Soviet states. The forces that it will inherit will require a substantial and concerted institutional, professional, and technological overhaul before it can once again become a formidable military establishment. Meanwhile, even the flexing of crippled Russian military power around its periphery should concern American policy makers, for there is always the potential for spillover into Europe, the Middle East, and Asia.

Similarly, the assembling of a Russian defense industrial establishment will require a stable political and economic environment and, most importantly, time. Given the extent of economic and institutional decay, a decade of dedicated effort is probably the minimum required to build the industrial foundation for rearmament.

When one begins to look out beyond a decade, however, all bets are off. Given enough motivation and time, Russia could assemble a significant military foundation. The key is motivation, because over time the shift to a smaller national military establishment will present the opportunity to eliminate many of the institutional ills that have plagued the Soviet armed forces since 1985. So the question is whether a succession of Russian governments over the next ten years or more will feel compelled to make the sacrifices to establish Russian military power.

Thus there is a window of opportunity to affect the tone and tenor of Russian national security policy and international behavior. Russia must come to feel that it has a stake in the peaceful and cooperative evolution in the international system. In this respect, the political forces for nonmilitarism within Russia have never been stronger.

Proliferation

A second concern falls under the generic heading of proliferation. Even if military power reemerges in the region as the currency of politics, there is a fear that the chaos and disintegration described above could result in the dispersion of dangerous weapons and capabilities to Third World states.

Nuclear Proliferation. First and foremost is the issue of nuclear weapons proliferation. What are the prospects that elements of the former Soviet nuclear arsenal might be spread around the globe? Unfortunately, this problem has been blown far out of proportion by simplistic mirror-imaging, extensive misinformation, and in some instances deliberate manipulation by interested parties in the former Soviet Union.

Briefly, no government among the post-Soviet states, except for Russia, has had physical custody of nuclear weapons. Nor has any even attempted to gain physical custody. Likewise, operational control over nuclear weapons has remained vested with the commonwealth armed forces—forces that answer to Russia. So, for all the loose talk about eleven, four, or two emerging nuclear powers, there is still only one.

Political, procedural, technical, and operational controls remain far stronger than is popularly believed. Press reports about missing nuclear weapons and smuggled fissile materials have all been false. (In some instances there has been confusion between the delivery vehicles and the nuclear weapons. For example, the bomber regiment in Ukraine that has been contemplating switching allegiance away from the commonwealth only controls aircraft. It does not have nuclear weapons.)

This does not mean, however, that it is impossible that one or even several nuclear weapons or, more likely, weapons components might "get lost." But this is a far cry from the handwringing and hyping that have surrounded the calls to save us from the alleged 27,000 loose Soviet nuclear weapons. Moreover, the risk of a major nuclear power plant accident somewhere in the former Soviet Union is considerably greater and the consequences far more hideous than those of such small-scale proliferation.

An associated nuclear proliferation risk emanates from "loose Soviet nuclear weapons experts." Some fear that, lacking alternative employment, a portion of the reputed 10,000 specialists will spill onto the world market. Here again, the possibility of a few such instances is real, but the threat has been blown out of all proportion.

While these elite Soviet scientists might be happy to move to the U.S. or Europe, they evince no interest in moving to wholly alien cultures and societies in the Third World. Strong social ties to family, friends, and country act to counter alleged economic incentives. The prospect of working on a primitive nuclear program is not a professional enticement. And there are strong professional and organizational forces keeping them in place.

Indeed, it is the desire to keep their research teams intact that has led many to turn to subtle extortion. "Either give us money for research, or we might go overseas." But very few, if any, are prepared to carry out that threat.

And even if some did choose to sell their services, their impact on nuclear proliferation would be marginal at best. Most prospective proliferants have more than enough scientific talent in-house. What they need are industrial engineers and production equipment. Soviet specialists have no knowledge of the international market nor any connections with foreign equipment suppliers. They would be of little net value to Third World regimes seeking nuclear weapons.

Conventional Arms Proliferation. The possibility of significant transfers of former Soviet conventional arms to the Third World comes from two sources. First, the post-Soviet states are sitting on large stocks of weapons for which they have little need or capability to maintain. At the same time, they are strapped for cash. A massive sell-off would seem to be in their interest. Second, the defense industries are desperately trying to save themselves. Foreign sales, as already described, is a survival strategy.

A fire sale of Soviet weapons stocks might have the immediate impact of boosting some Third World arsenals. It is doubtful, however, that it will really affect regional military balances or capabilities. After all, is there any evidence that the former Soviet Union withheld military technologies from its troublemaking client states? Didn't Iraq get all its Scud missiles from the Soviets? Didn't Syria get its air defense weapons, artillery, and tanks from the Soviets? Didn't Libya get its bombers from the Soviets? What prospective Third World beneficiary of a big sell-off is not already drowning in Soviet military equipment of dubious value? The impact of such a sale will be marginal at best.

The promise of massive foreign arms sales by entrepreneurial post-Soviet defense industries will probably never be realized. There are several reasons. First, the quality of post-Soviet weaponry will not match world standards for many years to come. The poor showing of Soviet-made weaponry in Iraq—irrespective of the real source of the blame—has colored international perceptions of their value. When Soviet weapons were given away or sold at subsidized prices in very large quantities, quality trade-offs were acceptable. But they will not prove to be so attractive in small numbers likely to be available in the future and not at "real" prices.

Perhaps more importantly, it is extremely unlikely that the post-Soviet defense industries will be able to provide the reliable and timely support and spare parts flow required to keep their clients happy. The most advanced Sukhoi fighter jets will not be of much use unless engine parts can be obtained as needed. Nor will legions of military advisors and technicians be available for free, as they were in the past.

There is also a tricky interrepublic political question confronting Russia and its neighbors. Russia holds about 70 percent of former Soviet defense industries. With the exception of small arms production, ammunition, artillery, and some limited military vehicle manufacturing, all of the other republics will require components and supplies from Russia to continue manufacturing traditional military goods. Will Russia want to help its potential competitors or will it prefer to sell on the international market itself—to the extent there is a market for post-Soviet arms?

Here again the marginal significance of arms sales on regional balances and capabilities should be considered. Can such sales ever match, let alone exceed, what the former Soviet Union attempted to do? The answer is no. Of course some specific weapons may be sold to specific countries that represent new capabilities—such as an attack submarine being sold to Iran—and such sales should raise red flags. But the net effect on international security will be far less than portrayed.

Regional Conflict

The potential for regional conflict has been amply demonstrated by Armenia and Azerbaijan and inside Georgia. Far greater are international concerns over a possible Russian-Ukrainian conflict. This is certainly understandable given the shaky state of their political relations and the intensity of their dispute over how to divide up the remnants of Soviet military power. Then, too, there are nuclear weapons on both territories.

It would be a mistake, however, to conclude that either country has a serious interest in conflict or that the disagreements over military forces are really about military issues. The ongoing disputes between Russia and Ukraine regarding the disposition of nuclear weapons, the Black Sea Fleet, and dividing up the remaining spoils of the Red Army represent political contests over sovereignty and liquidation rights. It should not be interpreted in military balance terms. Had the Soviet postal system survived, rather than its military, the two republics would be squabbling over mailboxes. To be sure, the risk of inadvertent conflict is always present, but it needs to be kept in perspective.

To conclude, it is not my intent to argue that there are no international security risks emanating from the breakup of the Soviet Union. Measured concern about nuclear security, arms proliferation, and regional conflict are justified. Policy making, however, will not be aided by greatly inflating the dangers posed or by artificially perpetuating a crisis atmosphere. We have the time and opportunity to formulate and implement deliberate policies that can ensure the cooperation of the post-Soviet states in producing a new international security environment.

Notes

[1] For a detailed discussion see Meyer (1991/1992).

[2] The interaction of all these effects was illustrated by an incident at a bomber base in Uzin, Ukraine. Orders were received from the commonwealth command to fly several aircraft to Russia. The officers refused, however, because the Ukrainian government had issued standing orders that no military equipment on Ukrainian soil was to move without Ukrainian authorization. Thus to fly the planes out would violate legitimate political authorities, and to remain at base would violate legitimate political authorities.

Most significantly, most of the officers at the base eventually swore allegiance to Ukraine out of fear of being transferred back to Russia, where housing and living standards were notably worse. Patriotism and national identity were not at issue. See Serge Schmemann, "Friction Rises as Ukraine and Russia Clash over Ex-Soviet Armed Forces," *New York Times*, March 3, 1992, p. 3.

[3] The multiple reasons why this is the inevitable outcome are too lengthy to detail in this chapter. They are basically tied to the inherent inability of Belarus, Ukraine, or Kazakhstan to operate and maintain the strategic systems on their territories for any consequential length of time.

⁴ This type of stockpiling was a classic feature of the old system. It was an adaptive response to the tautness of the monopoly supply structure that existed. Many plants would stockpile one or more years' worth of input components as insurance.

⁵ Somewhat ominously there is great interest in acquiring dual-use technologies. Interestingly, the development of dual-use technologies was the major thrust of the VPK conversion plan.

5

Foreign Policy

ROBERT LEGVOLD

G orbachev invented the all-consuming domestic political agenda, and passed it on to his many successors. As in the last two years of his power, foreign policy for the new states possesses near inconsequence, at least foreign policy as anything other than domestic imperative by another name. Writing about Ukrainian foreign policy or Uzbek foreign policy or even Russian foreign policy, therefore, is rather like studying shadows, as I will describe in a moment. Yet, at the same time, an enormously complex and potentially unsettling system of foreign relations has begun to take shape in the area of the former Soviet Union, one capable of exporting much stress and confusion into the larger international setting.

ROBERT LEGVOLD is a professor of political science at Columbia University. He was the director of The Harriman Institute from the fall of 1986 through the spring of 1992. Prior to coming to The Harriman Institute as its associate director in 1984, he served for six years as senior fellow and director of the Soviet Studies Project at the Council on Foreign Relations in New York. For most of the preceding decade, he was on the faculty of Tufts University, and today serves on its Board of Trustees.

After the floodgates of 1989 opened, few people in the Soviet Union or in the West any longer could have, had they tried, described in broad and coherent terms Soviet foreign policy. Officials working with their Soviet counterparts on the Middle East problem knew where the Soviets stood on a specific issue of this sort, and on a Cambodian settlement, or on an arms control accord in Europe. But ask about the larger thrust of Soviet policy—its basic themes, its overall strategic design, or even its relative order of priorities—and you would not have gotten much of an answer. Still more astonishingly, particularly in the United States where for forty years such matters had been preoccupying, no one really cared. In the two years from 1989 to 1991, the issue had ceased to be Soviet behavior abroad, displaced by a larger concern over the vagaries of reforming Soviet society. We stopped worrying about what mischief the Soviet Union might do in the outside world and substituted a new apprehension over the perils that might befall the country, especially if others were likely to suffer as a result.

Back in the Soviet Union, a collapsing economy and a looming crisis of the nation-state swamped normal foreign policy concerns. Understandably Mikhail Gorbachev and his government, faced with primal threats of this order, had little time or energy to worry about sweeping foreign policy visions or even about the overall coherence of their country's engagement abroad.

Soviet foreign policy, however, had lost its shape and depth for more than this reason alone. In a sense the domestic crisis that so thoroughly eclipsed Soviet thinking about the outside world formed part of a more devastating whole. Truth is, between 1989 and 1991 the Soviet Union ceased to be a superpower, and, while the decline at home constituted much of the reason, far more was involved. By 1990–91 the Soviet position in international politics, as conceived by all postwar Soviet leaders, had crumbled. No longer did the Soviet Union lead a cohesive bloc, let alone one said to be history's grand alternative. No longer did it enjoy the backing of a European alliance. No longer could it compete with the United States or anyone else of means in the far reaches of the globe. No longer was it even the most powerful or consequential actor close to home in Europe and East Asia. Overnight the Soviet

Union had become, at best, a regional power—one with enormous, diverting domestic problems. In the world beyond its borders, as in the 1920s and 1930s, it was, again, a "price taker." When Gorbachev began his foreign policy revolution in 1985–86, the revolution that so transformed the prevailing international order, he thought that he was refurbishing and modernizing a superpower's foreign policy. He had no time, even less the freedom, to deal with the consequences of a vastly different outcome, to recast his ideas, to plan the policy of a regional power, albeit one stretching across a continent that intersected several regions. This problem, along with many others, was left to those who came after.

Those who came after, for the most part, start with no confusion on this score: their states are regional powers with few of the pretensions or prospects of the Soviet Union. I say "for the most part," because Russia clouds the issue in ways to which I will return. They are regional powers with enormous, diverting domestic problems. They, even less than the Soviet Union near its death, can release themselves from the iron grip of internal imperatives—destitute economies, half-formed political orders, demoralized publics, and the centrifugal force of restless ethnic groupings. Foreign policy for their leaders derives directly and implacably from the mess they are in at home. Thus the Soviet Union began and ended with foreign policy as the poor and bedraggled stepchild of internal convulsion. Such is the beginning of the new states.

In a more fundamental sense, however, the condition or situation of foreign policy in the new states stands in sharp contrast to that of most postwar Soviet foreign policy. The utter subordination to domestic need already distinguishes it from a time when ambitions abroad were pursued without much regard for conditions at home. From there, the entire scheme of policy, the entire order of priority has been turned upside down. Where the postwar Soviet Union started from a global perspective, and, like the United States, came instinctively to judge developments in any part of the world by their likely larger ramifications, particularly for the country's overall position, the new states start from their relations with one another. Ninety percent of what Leonid Kravchuk has on his mind, when it comes to foreign policy, is Russia and the other former republics. The same applies to his counterparts, including Boris Yeltsin. Then, in ever widening concentric circles, they raise their eyes to focus on their immediate neighborhoods—Europe, for the Ukrainians, Belarusians, and Moldovans; Turkey, Iran, and the rest of the Muslim world, for the Azerbaijanis and Central Asians; East Asia and Europe, for the Russians; and an uncertain concatenation for the Georgians and Armenians. Somewhere in the distance stands the rest of the world, materialized largely as international economic institutions and aid-giving nations.

Lately some of the Russian foreign policy leadership has shown signs of wishing this could be different. Andrei Kozyrev, Russia's bright, liberal foreign minister, while in southern Africa in February 1992, referred to the Soviet Union's original contribution to the Angolan settlement as the basis for "the continuation of our global role." " 'Superpower,' " he confessed, is not a label he much likes, "nevertheless, it applies, considering our responsibility to the world." The fact that the Russian foreign minister was this far from home this early in the life of an independent Russia already said a good deal about the urge to be seen as a major player on a global scale. Some of the same, presumably, explained the Russians' eagerness to host a round of the Mid-East peace talks a few weeks earlier.

It is, however, a confused sentiment, out of phase with another deeper dimension of the problem: Russia, like the other post-Soviet states, must, before settling on an international vocation, first struggle with the underlying matter of self-identity. "How can Russia know what its foreign policy should be," as one of the top aides of Alexander Yakovlev, a senior figure in the Gorbachev leadership, asked me, "until it knows what Russia is?" The process of sorting out national identity, of course, is not an easy task to be settled in parliamentary deliberation, a weekend convention, or presidential decrees. It goes to the heart of nation building, the underlying challenge facing all the new states, including Russia.

Inchoate Foreign Policies

To some degree the problem can be seen in key institutions, such as the Russian Foreign Ministry, which early on tended to divide along two lines. Many of the professionals retained from the old Soviet ministry favored a foreign policy agenda more or less similar to the one set by Gorbachev and Shevardnadze. It featured the United States, the arms control enterprises of the last twenty years, and a wide array of Soviet, now Russian, international responsibilities. The last, to be sure, they would have approached with still greater restraint and moderation than Gorbachev and his people. The other part of the Foreign Ministry—primarily those who originally formed the Russian republic's Foreign Ministry— had broken with this scheme of things, and would have ostentatiously severed ties with former radical clients, stressed relations with the former Soviet republics and important neighbors, such as Germany and Japan, and labored to have Russia accepted as a normal, law-abiding European nation.[1] For both, however, a democratic Russia, at peace with itself, served as the premise of the policies they advocated.

Others start from more elemental positions. At root are differences over whether Russia ought to seek its destiny among the other Slavic republics or whether Russia's future lies with broader parts of the former Soviet Union, including, in particular, Central Asia. The contrast snakes through the Russian government up to the highest levels and well across the Russian parliament. Except for a radical fringe, few on either side have in mind a restored union, Slavic or otherwise (although before the Soviet flag was lowered for the last time, hardly any in the first group could have imagined Russia without Ukraine and Belarus, and hardly any in the second group would have worried about making a choice between one or another part of the country). Rather they differ over the issue of where Russia should invest itself: whether to concentrate its energies—and ultimately its identity—on one set of culturally linked states or more broadly in ways reflecting a more generous notion of what Russia should strive to be.

At some deep, historical-psychological level, Dostoevski's notion that, in Asia, Russians are regarded as Europeans, and, in

Europe, as Asiatics (he said, Tatars) may be resurfacing, but in this case with significant foreign policy implications.[2] Those, for example, whose emotions and political instincts lean toward the Slavic core tend to look westward. With the exception of Japan, which they think of as part of the West, other regions of the world are of secondary interest.[3] Those in the other category tend either to see Russia's destiny as much, if not more, in Asia than Europe, or to imagine Russia as a country transcending cultural or political alignments, standing apart from its immediate environment, much as Great Britain did in the eighteenth and nineteenth centuries. Some of the intellectuals who hold to this last view would even have Russia take on Britain's earlier role as balancer within the international system.

There is, yet, a third current stirring in the politics of Russia, particularly among the new, often youthful politicians in parliament. They are indifferent to much of the outside world, have little knowledge of it, and concentrate their energies and hopes on the problems they see before them within their own country. They have no particular interest in thinking about any kind of an international role for Russia, and, when they exert their influence, it is often to turn away from commitments and involvements abroad.

For the other new states, the problem of underlying identity is every bit as vexed. Most of the Central Asians feel little affinity for Russia or her sister Slav states; culturally they are drawn to the south. But after 125 years of colonialism, they have been welded into a "Russian order," and can ill-afford to find their identity entirely elsewhere. They are also ruled by elites who greatly fear the impact of Islam on their societies, should they become too much a part of the Muslim world. Nursultan Nazarbaev, the leader of Kazakhstan, a country that has never existed before, and where large chunks of territory have been settled by the Russians, leaving the Kazakhs a minority in their own land, reflects the tensions among the choices he and his people must make. At a press conference in Austria in early 1992, Nazarbaev underscored Kazakhstan *and Russia's* special responsibility for shielding Central Asia from Muslim fundamentalism and Iran. Yet, at every turn, Kazakhstan's representatives join the other Central Asians at the convocations of the Muslim states to the south, and, when Nazarbaev travels abroad, usually he heads in the same direction. To make matters worse, Nazarbaev casts his country in the role of a bridge between Asia and Europe, a nonsensical idea that he compounds by proposing Kazakhstan for eventual membership in the European Community, and further compounds by threatening to join unspecified Arab or Asian unions if thwarted.

To the west, Belarus suffers an even more fundamental problem: other than Russia, no republic was more integrally a part of the Soviet Union than Byelorussia, not the least, because no other region was more integrally a part of Imperial Russia. Belarus has a long history, but none of it as an independent state, not even in the post-1917 period, when many fragments of the empire briefly tasted freedom. Nor during the Gorbachev era did Belarusian elites—even dissident elites—fancy the prospect of independence, and begin the struggle for it. Independence is a wondrous, intimidating surprise.

Belarus underscores a fundamental point. The collapse of the Soviet Empire is not like the collapse of the British Empire nor even the more frequently cited comparison, the collapse of the Ottoman and Austro-Hungarian Empires. And Belarus is not like a newly decolonized India or Nigeria, societies intact and only partly penetrated by the political graftings of British imperialism. Belarus thoroughly embodies the imperial system of which it has been a part since Catherine's time. Nor does it resemble the first Czechoslovak republic, created after World War I, an invention free of the overshadowing power of a large, lingering core state. More than economic dependency will make it hard for Belarusian leaders to draw away from the Russian orbit.

Even Ukraine, blessed with land and people—a proud people determined to make the most of independence—will not find its place in the larger world without a struggle. On the surface, the choice is made: Ukraine means to be an integral part of the new Europe, as democratic as any other state, as fully marketized. But its leaders know this will not happen by tomorrow, not merely because Germany, France, and the other members of the European Community already have their hands full with Poland, Hungary, and Czechoslovakia, not merely because the artifacts of the Soviet period lay like heavy bonds, but because, for a thousand years, Ukrainian and Russian identities have mixed inextricably.

Ukrainians, beginning with Leonid Kravchuk, understand what all this means. Their country will not soon merge with the currents remaking the political and economic life of Western Europe. For this reason, Kravchuk often speaks of Ukraine as at the center of Europe, "on the crossroads of the main East-West highways," by which he apparently means at the intersection of the remainder of Europe with the former Soviet Union. To suit this strategic circumstance, he then grandly declares Ukraine will be both neutral and nonnuclear. But no one in that country really wants to be left hanging somewhere between the old East and the new West, and, if it cannot be avoided, then, as rising voices argue, let it not be without very special (nuclear) forms of protection.

The crux of the problem, of course, is Russia. For the moment, Ukraine strains not merely to put distance between itself and a repudiated Soviet past, but to disentangle itself from a millennium of Russian history. Out of this almost surely unavailing struggle, one goal emerges to dominate all others: the quest for independence. The primary order of business is to make Ukraine genuinely independent, first, in the eyes of the outside world, particularly in Russian eyes and, second, in the minds of Ukrainians, particularly of Ukrainian politicians and elites.

All this goes a long way toward explaining Ukrainian attitudes toward the Commonwealth of Independent States (CIS). Despite appearances, Kravchuk and people like him do not deny the underlying need for a commonwealth. Ukrainians may want to be a part of Europe's dynamic half, but, as many understand, their destiny is with their fellow former Soviet republics. The commonwealth they favor, however, is not the Commonwealth of Independent States, a residue of the collapsed Soviet Union, but a commonwealth of independent states, built from the ground up by constituent states that have themselves been critically transformed internally and externally.

In a revealing allusion, Kravchuk has said that Ukraine's model is democratic France.[4] He means Gaullist France, a nation that knew how to stand up for itself against imposing allies. He thinks of the French model, one guesses, not as a representation of Ukraine in Europe, but as a symbol of Ukraine within the family of post-

Soviet countries. When he and other Ukrainian leaders speak of a nonnuclear and neutral Ukraine, this is the kind of neutrality they have in mind. (It sets one to wondering about the sturdiness of the nonnuclear component.)

The trouble is, as Ukrainian leaders well understand, their future and that of comity among the former Soviet republics depend on the course of Ukrainian-Russian relations. Even if these unfold according to the happiest analogy considered by thoughtful Ukrainians—that of U.S.–Canadian relations—the implications for the "French model" give pause. Ukraine is not likely to play the United States to Russia's Canada.[5] The unhappiest analogy, also on the minds of Ukrainians, the current relationship between Siberia and Croatia, or even embittered relations short of open conflict would be even harder on the "French model." Poland between the wars, a country on its own, without an answer to the dangers beyond its borders, would be more like it.

If the prior questions facing the new states are so fundamental, it should come as no surprise that the conceptual base of foreign policy remains—to be charitable—undeveloped. Everywhere, Russia partially excepted, national leaders are struggling to enter the international political arena without a coherent set of ideas to guide them, and virtually no sense of how to formulate one. They substitute random attributes for ideas—largely, one senses, because these signify sovereignty or accompany membership in the international club. When, for example, in October 1991, the Belarusian parliament issued a "Statement on the Principles of the Foreign Policy of Belarus," the content was a string of organizations and conventions to be joined or accepted. To this was appended a single appeal in favor of transforming the "European continent" into "a nuclear weapon–free zone."

In December 1991, Anatoly Zlenko, the Ukrainian foreign minister, too, elaborated the main principles of his country's foreign policy.[6] Again, he offered a scattered list. Two items touched on previous Soviet obligations that Ukraine would assume and in what measure, but named only one, that of the external Soviet debt. Two expressed Kiev's position on a national army and nuclear weapons. Two declared Ukraine's intention "to become an equal participant in the general European process," as a nuclear-

free state outside military blocs. Point seven, the final item on the
list, stressed Ukraine's determination to preserve its territory as
"indivisible and inviolable," and promised to respect the same
principle in dealing with others. Zlenko, on this occasion, of course
was not attempting to outline the defining features of Ukrainian
foreign policy. But neither has anyone since.

To be fair, all of the new states, with the exception of Russia,
have few resources from which to fashion a foreign policy. In none
of them, again, save for Russia, does anything like a reasonable
number of diplomats, scholars, and journalists knowledgeable
about international affairs exist. In fact, in most of them, except
Ukraine, the numbers can be counted on one or two hands. Even
Belarus began the process of constructing a policy-making apparatus and staffing embassies around the world with a Foreign Ministry of approximately thirty people. Most of the others started with
even less.

Having a far larger and more experienced foreign policy community, Russia, as might be expected, has done somewhat better.
Kozyrev, on occasion, has sketched a number of basic ideas that
could theoretically serve to orient Russian foreign policy, were
they to prevail within Yeltsin's government. In November 1991 in
a presentation to the International Institute of Strategic Studies in
London, he called for the states of the "northern hemisphere" to
form a political and military union, and Yeltsin has since talked
about a "democratic zone of trust, cooperation, and security,"
forming "across the northern hemisphere."[7] Neither man means
to suggest that the north should band together against the other
half of the international community, but Kozyrev apparently believes that Russia should, as its central goal, seek a place in the
West by helping to revamp in still more radical ways military
relationships among the powerful. When he is challenged by critics who complain that this will only add to the U.S. advantage and
leave Russia more vulnerable to *diktat*, he responds with what is
doubtless another very different principle on which to base Russian foreign and defense policy: "We ourselves," he says, "threaten
no one, and we take as our point of departure that no developed,
democratic, civilian society, where reasonable, rational principle
prevails, can threaten us."[8] The unfinished end to the sentence

would appear to be "no matter what the state of the military balance."

Kozyrev is an idealist, far more so than many of his prominent political colleagues. He is also conceptually far more sophisticated than most of them, including Yeltsin. So it would be wrong to assume that his ideas are the ideas that underpin Russian foreign policy. On the contrary the evidence suggests that thinking at this level floats somewhere beyond their consciousness.[9] But it matters that it exists at all, and that shreds of it show up in Yeltsin's speeches as well as in Russian diplomatic initiatives.

Thus as those of us on the outside, whether analysts or policy makers, try to come to grips with the challenges likely to emerge from this region, the first step is to understand the confounded base of foreign policy. For the most part, these are not countries that yet know their place in the outside world or even how to create an adequate framework for wrestling with the problem. They are, by and large, as innocent of the mechanics, modalities, institutions, and practices of international politics as the rawest newly independent states, whether in the first, post-1948 wave or in the second, post-1960 one. For this reason alone, we should assume that a greatly fluid period lies ahead. The altered contours and rhythms to be imposed on the larger international order by this part of the world will not be settled soon.

A Fragile Milieu

Still, history marches on. With or without conscious, organized human intervention, new realities are being created daily. They are the product of the dynamic among these states and of them with the world beyond. In short, with or without a conscious, coherent design, there is foreign policy in this region, or rather foreign policy behavior, behavior with consequences. I will come back to these consequences and their potential implications for the West, after first looking at the dynamic behind them.

To repeat, as these new states take up roles in the international community—some of them timidly and with great uncertainty, others readily and with verve—they are scarcely captains of their own fate. In the battle, foreign policy is not so much a carefully calibrated instrument in the hands of purposeful regimes working from well-defined, coherent, comprehensive agendas as the residual of internal turbulence, crises, and imperatives.

The effect of this turbulence, these crises, and these imperatives, as I have said, is, first, to reverse the focus of policy geographically from one that was broad-to-narrow, starting with salient global developments, to one that is narrow-to-broad, starting with inter-republican relations. But, second, and even more important, the effect is to swell the inner concentric circle, the narrowest circle of relations, all out of proportion. These are regional states practicing regional strategies only if one operates with a narrow definition of region.

The third effect is to skew priorities among foreign policy issues. Political scientists and politicians often repeat that in today's world the dividing line between domestic and foreign policy issues has been thoroughly effaced. In the former Soviet Union, however, one has become the other. This is because matters that were indisputably ones of domestic politics are now indisputably matters of international politics, assuming in the process a very different character. It does not happen every day that a nation-state turns into an international subsystem.

Domestic politics have become international politics, of course, because of the collapse of empire. This collapse has given rise to two sorts of phenomena, and together they overwhelm the foreign policy agendas of the new states. Their only rival is the need to enlist the outside world in the struggle against economic ruin and for economic reform.

Liquidating the Soviet Union and its holdings constitutes the first of the two. The question of who gets what after a death often complicates relations among survivors, and almost always, when there is no last will and testament to guide decisions. In this case, the problem of *the* successor state adds a further complication. From debt to naval frigates, Russia, Ukraine, and their fellow former republics are spending enormous time and energy arguing over the division of the estate, for understandable reasons. After all, if the politics of resource allocation can be intense within a single political entity, where a sovereign state arbitrates, asset distribution in the anarchy of international politics is a good deal more so.

Western policy makers whose days are consumed with monitoring export control regimes, preventing the proliferation of nuclear weapons, negotiating orderly marketing arrangements, answering for UN special fund arrears, generating refugee assistance, and the like can only imagine what life must be like for policy makers whose foreign policy agenda starts with the task of dividing up an army of 3.7 million with 27,000 nuclear warheads, a debt of $80 billion, the world's largest scientific establishment, the costs of Chernobyl and untold other environmental disasters, memberships in 5,000 organizations, 15,000 treaty obligations, Aeroflot's 7,200 aircraft and 3,700 offices, gold and hard-currency reserves, a national space program, and much more. Since the process profoundly affects the material base on which leaderships hope to build their nations, the stakes are very high.

Were there a chance the distribution could be equitably done, the sheer complexity of doing it would create trouble enough. When no such chance exists, when one state is bound to end up with the lion's share of everything, the problem takes on an added dimension. It starts on a point of principle: Russia insists that it is the full and complete successor state to the Soviet Union—the "continuation" state, to use the technical phrase; most of the others, led by Ukraine, with equal fervor disagree. Willy nilly, however, the Russians are having their way, not the least because much of the international community finds it convenient to concentrate most of the rights and duties of the former superpower in one set of hands. But, along the way, relations among the new states suffer, in the process jeopardizing larger considerations, such as the prospects of integration.

The issue dots the foreign policies of these states in a hundred different ways. It is not merely the obvious discontents, as when Kravchuk protests the Russians' taking over Soviet embassies around the world or his making a move on the Black Sea Fleet. It is also there when Nazarbaev criticizes Yeltsin for implicitly assuming that he speaks for Kazakhstan, Ukraine, and Belarus in proposing to the Americans specific further deep cuts in nuclear arms or when the Ukrainians importune international financial institutions to block Russia's claim to Soviet assets.

Tensions arising out of disagreements over the distribution of Soviet property and entitlements, however, are only one side of the issue. The collapse of empire affects foreign policy in a second, more consuming fashion—largely because the collapse and its echoes have not ended. The dominant trend in this region remains disintegration. Old political institutions and economic forms are still coming apart; the Commonwealth of Independent States is not so much a mechanism for integration as a means of regulating the disintegration, and itself a likely victim; and even within states, such as Russia, the centrifugal forces of nationalism and ethnic rebellion continue to build.

The dynamic this gives to international politics among the new states is friction-filled and unstable. Because few of them are genuinely nation-states, in the sense of commanding the clear, conscious loyalty of nearly all inhabitants, anything in the behavior of others that casts a shadow stirs anger. One sees the phenomenon at work in Nazarbaev's sharply critical letters to Yeltsin in fall 1990, when the Cossacks of western Kazakhstan, Russian flags lofted, marked the 400th anniversary of their service to the Russian state, and Moscow did nothing to discourage "a blatant disrespect for the state sovereignty" of Kazakhstan.[10] The fuss continued for weeks, with Nazarbaev eventually suggesting that Yeltsin and his people viewed the Ural Cossacks as a way "to control Kazakh affairs."

The same can be said of Kravchuk's petulant public rejoinders, when asked about the Russians. It is time for them, he has said, to stop thinking about Ukraine as part of Russia, time to stop the "younger brother, older brother" routine, and time to stop treating Ukrainian independence as misbehavior.[11] Such "great power chauvinism," he adds for good measure, simply "brings out the national protest in us." Nearly everywhere, the same prickliness prevails, and for the same reason. Georgians resent any hint that Ossetians identify more closely with peoples on the other side of the border, and charge the Russians with egging the wrong people on. Ukrainians bristle at political parties in Czechoslovakia for giving encouragement to the secessionist sentiments of portions of the population in Zakarpattya.

The flip side of this problem is the immense and dangerous issue of the diasporas, 60 million people, 26 million of them Russian, often constituting between 25 and 40 percent of the population in

other states. Where trouble would be the most explosive, between
Russia and Ukraine—for the Russians in Ukraine number 11 out
of 52 million—restraint and common sense stifle any serious friction. But almost everywhere else, the question of the treatment of,
grievances of, or alternatively, aggressiveness of the Russians in
states other than their own occupies—often preoccupies—Moscow in its dealings with former sister republics.

Its corroding effect much of the time is straightforward and
unmistakable. At other times it works its effect more subtly, but
with devastating consequence. When Catherine Lalumière, secretary general of the Council on Europe, on a visit to the Baltic states
in March 1992, appeared to condone Latvia and Estonia's discriminatory legislation against Russian "aliens," she did more
than incense Russian parliamentarians back in Moscow. Her performance triggered a cascade of complaints against the liberal
foreign policy of Yeltsin and Kozyrev, most notably among nor-
mally supportive elements.

It was as though this one affront placed in relief the many other
insults and disappointments for which people now blamed
Russia's new foreign policy, a policy seen increasingly as naive and
weak. Within the foreign policy community, and even within the
Foreign Ministry itself, voices mocked the Russian leadership's
fixation on returning the country to the fold of "civilized nations,"
its readiness to turn the other cheek and sacrifice national interest
simply to gain the good will of Western governments, governments
that were not likely to reciprocate with economic help or even
respect. "Rosy dreams of a rose-bedecked 'return to civilization'
from 'communist barbarism' had ended" was the summary of the
mood at one conference sponsored by the Foreign Ministry.[12]
Kozyrev's friends and supporters, not primitive Russian nationalists, were tiring of the "sickeningly sweet" themes, the concession-
ary disarmament proposals, and the tolerated "scorn" of Western
politicians. Unless Russia began to stand up for itself, they argued,
politicians more open to confrontation would have their day, and
the people would follow.

For the moment, the issue of national minorities hangs like a
specter, requiring a steady foreign policy hand, but it has not yet
begun to ruin relations between states and to consume foreign

policies, with the ominous exception of the conflict between Armenia and Azerbaijan. Still the danger is never far away, and political leaders in several countries, most worryingly in Russia, have done less than they should to keep the issue contained. Were the political scene to grow ugly, particularly in Russia, and open the way to those who deal in the excesses of nationalism, tension in the region could turn deadly with discouraging speed.

Thus the outsider must add to the rudimentary character of policy discussed earlier the fragility of the milieu within which policy operates. Where the forces of disintegration prevail, the essential quality of international politics can change rapidly and profoundly. There are in the post-Soviet interrepublican milieu too many sources of instability, and should they intensify or begin to interact, they can in short order transform a comparatively stable environment into a fundamentally unstable and violent one.

These sources of instability, because they are intertwined, carry in them a destructive synergy. Border disputes and territorial irredentism, for example, frequently derive from or contribute to conflicts over national minorities. The Russian parliament's efforts to force the issue of Khrushchev's gift of the Crimea to Ukraine in 1954 has long ceased to be a frivolous matter. The first flickers of Lithuanian interest in absorbing the Kaliningrad oblast provoked an instant and stern official Russian reaction. In both instances, nothing untoward is likely to happen as long as the local Russian majority continues not to want Moscow's radical intervention. If that changes, the situation overnight would present a different magnitude of trouble.

Not a single one of the fifteen successor states escapes being either the object or the protagonist of territorial irredenta. Ukraine has seven borders, three of which are openly challenged by other governments (Russia, Rumania, and Moldova), and two more of which are implicitly contested by groups either inside or outside Ukraine (Czechoslovakia and Belarus). Scarcely any of the new states exist within clear and unquestioned borders. Thus it would be imprudent in the extreme for them or us to rule out an evolution toward a different and far more threatening context.

Finally, the foreign policy agendas of the new states are further skewed by the disastrous economic plight of all of these states and their need to seek, and, if necessary, to compete for the assistance of the outside world. Not surprisingly, none of them—even Russia—can afford a balanced or comprehensive foreign policy. To expect them to do their part in devising and bringing about solutions to major international problems or even to give more than fleeting attention to the process of strengthening security regimes in Central Europe and East Asia is not realistic. For the most part, national leaders have their minds only on the massive economic problems at home. When they travel abroad or receive foreign leaders, whatever the other subjects touched upon, they are thinking primarily about trade, aid, and investment.

The Outside World and Post-Soviet Disintegration

In many respects, for the West, too, the ongoing effects of disintegration in this region produce most of what matters. Much of it is obvious. If, for example, the low-level and sporadic conflicts of the moment escalate into violence involving Russia, Ukraine, or any of the other larger republics, Europe's and presumably the United States' peace of mind will suffer. Conflict either between any two major entities or within any one of them will doubtless be unsettling elsewhere. Violence or merely the continued degradation of economies could send hundreds of thousands of people fleeing toward the already strained societies of Eastern Europe.

Economic disintegration also pushes Russia and other republics with sizable defense sectors to promote arms sales to third countries. Yeltsin is on record defending his country's decision to maintain, even to increase, arms exports as the only way to prevent the collapse of military industry, which would put millions out of work and lead to "social tensions." Russian Deputy Minister of Economy and Finances Ivan Materov has estimated that these sales will reach $8 billion in 1992, a larger sum than exported by the entire USSR the year before. Other of Yeltsin's advisors have called for an increase in Russia's quota of world uranium sales from 5 to 20 percent. Each week brings reports of noteworthy sales of arms and aircraft by one of the new states. In late February 1992 the Russian air force was authorized to put 1,600 aircraft on the market. A few

ter Kazakhstan announced plans to sell military equip-
hat included SU-24 bombers. Parts of the Black Sea Fleet
for sale, indeed, perhaps as many as fifty vessels, among them
ers and submarines. As Stephen Meyer points out in chapter
4, selling off the Soviet arsenal scarcely means that the new states
will be able to create modern arms-exporting industries. But over
the next several years the impact on international politics is not
likely to be any less.

Second, the effects of disintegration directly impinge on the
structure of military balances, threatening to complicate the task of
constructing safer and sounder security regimes in Central Europe
and South Asia. The risk of nuclear proliferation within the area of
the former Soviet Union is a case in point. Despite assurances on
which U.S. and other Western leaders are counting, there is a
chance that in the end, more than Russia will retain nuclear weapons. Nazarbaev has made increasingly plain his determination to
hang on to nuclear weapons as long as other powers in the region,
including China, have not eliminated theirs, and he talks about
Kazakhstan as sharing nuclear status with Russia.

Ukraine, for the moment, insists that its goal remains to become
nonnuclear by 1994, but its decision in March 1992 to halt in
midstream the transfer of short-range systems to Russia is not
reassuring. The underlying motive may have been to get the attention of the West or, more specifically, to pressure the United States
and other technologically advanced countries into providing
Ukraine with modern facilities for disposing of nuclear warheads
and the nuclear debris of Chernobyl, but the stated reason was to
avoid adding to the nuclear strength of Russia. It is but a small step
from wanting to deny Russia nuclear arms to wanting to balance
Russia's nuclear strength with weapons of one's own. Nor is it
self-evident that when the time for the choice comes, Kiev will find
it easy to give up the claim to special status in international affairs
conferred by strategic arms, particularly when that status is retained by what is increasingly regarded as an overweening neighbor.

Perhaps Meyer and other experts who know the technical characteristics of the Soviet strategic arsenal are right: only Russia will
be able to sustain a nuclear establishment, and Kazakhstan's

claims and Ukraine's vacillations are only so much posturing. Leaders in both countries obviously have come to appreciate the political cachet that nuclear weapons provide. There are Western embassies in Alma Ata (rather than Tashkent) that would not otherwise be there, and Kiev has discovered the one sure way to arouse Western interest in Ukraine is by agitating the nuclear issue. But then, at a minimum, international relations will at times be disturbed by these political manipulations. And, at a maximum, there remains the danger that ways will be found to preserve some kind of nuclear capability, no matter how rudimentary.

Even more the breakup of the Soviet Union has replaced a single, overpowering Red Army with a series of national armies, adding players to existing regional military balances, some of them, such as Russia and Ukraine, with a good deal more military power than their neighbors. Moreover, as the Soviet military fragments into large, albeit uneven pieces, already uneasy relationships, such as between Russia and Ukraine, are made more so. In the process, new complications are introduced into the effort to regulate the European arms balance. At the moment, for example, Russia balks at the notion that Ukraine would in theory, if the levels set by the conventional forces in Europe (CFE) agreement are upheld, retain stronger conventional forces than Russia west of the Urals.

And behind the potential problems raised for the broader European military balance by the collapse of Soviet military power lurks the new problem of managing and emerging military balance within the former Soviet Union. As Andrei Kortunov wisely notes, the issue in doubt is whether this balance, particularly on the European side of the old USSR, can and will be crafted in ways ensuring that "no non-Russian republic feels threatened, and Russia, in turn, does not feel isolated."[13] Or will instead the general pressures of disintegration and the parallel tendency on the part of the new states to deal unilaterally with anticipated security threats not in the end produce destabilizing defense choices?

Third, the disintegration of the Soviet Union has not only destroyed the integrity of what was once a solid geographical space, it has opened this territory to the politics of neighboring regions. At the four corners of the former empire, governments are hastening to position themselves, sometimes in hopes of satisfying long-held political aspirations, as Rumania in entering Moldovan politics over the question of Moldova's independence or reintegration into Rumania. Sometimes the foray owes more to narrow national concerns, as when Poland rushes to protect Poles in Lithuania, and Hungary, Hungarians in Ukraine. Sometimes it is driven by ambition and a sense of opportunity, such as Turkey and Iran's eager push for influence in Transcaucasia and Central Asia.

No area better illustrates how swiftly parts of the Soviet Union have become extensions of the international politics of other regions than Transcaucasia and Central Asia. There are, spread across these territories, more than 54 million Muslim peoples, and as they struggle to find their future, every country to the south, from Turkey to India, has developed a sudden and intense interest in them. They come bearing aid, in the case of Iran, $500 million to date, seeking to create the infrastructure for their influence, and in quest of many different things from religious converts to nuclear weapons.

The primary competitors appear to be Turkey and Iran, each hastening to get a step on the other, each seeing the region as critical to its aspirations of dominating either an Islamic bloc or a renewed pan-Turkic sphere. Both have already invested considerably in the region. Turkey has aided Azerbaijan's upgrade of its telecommunications system, and promised assistance to Kazakhstan, Uzbekistan, and Turkmenistan in modernizing their transportation facilities.[14] Iran is making Uzbekistan's capital, Tashkent, the focus of its Asia air operations, developing joint energy undertakings in Turkmenistan and Azerbaijan, and helping to set up a regional banking network. It has created a special government department to coordinate its initiatives in the area, and opened missions throughout the region. It, too, has quickly moved to create telecommunications links with part of the area, particularly with Persian-speaking Tajikistan, and air and sea links with Kazakhstan.

Despite the underlying competition, however—a competition that some in the West, beginning with the United States, hope will make Turkey a counterpoise to Iranian influence—the two countries have not been entirely at odds. Some argue that they in fact cooperate to a degree on policy in the region as well as in Afghanistan, Palestine, and Kurdistan.[15] Thus, for example, Turkey may not be much troubled by the Iranian foreign minister's active mediation in February and March 1992 between Azerbaijan and Armenia over the Nagorno-Karabakh conflict, all the more so that Turkey's own access to the region is impeded by the conflict, a conflict that it cannot do much to settle, given its own neuralgic relationship with Armenia.

Long-term Turkish-Iranian rivalry in the area, however, is but one important element in a complex dynamic of competition. Iran's offensive immediately brings in Saudi Arabia and other Arab states as well. The Saudis have come with money ($1.9 billion) to cover an ambitious program of religious education and support for their preferred religious societies, and direct investment, including new banks in several Central Asia countries.

Across the Hindu Kush, the fear of new Muslim allies for Pakistan stirs Indian anxiety. Doubtless the concern is not softened when India's leaders hear Pakistani politicians reporting on Kazakhstan's willingness to aid Pakistan with (peaceful) nuclear technology. In the winter of 1992 Nazarbaev traveled to Delhi to reassure Indian leaders of his country's determination to steer clear of Muslim alignments. (In general, he sought to create the impression that Kazakhstan would work to overcome divisions within the larger region, a message conveyed by the itinerary itself: Delhi, Islamabad, and Beijing.) But, Kazakh diplomacy notwithstanding, the Indian-Pakistani competition is inevitably swinging northward.

For now, however, the gravest complication for Central Asia's emergence from the ruins of the Soviet Union arises in the north, not the south. Because the process of disintegration has not stopped, but invaded the countries emerging out of the fallen Soviet Union, Russia threatens to come apart under the pressure of a combination of regional nationalisms and economic Balkanization. Most of the major national challenges—in Tatarstan, Bashkorstan, Chechen-Ingushetia, and beyond—involve complex political lineups influenced by sizable Muslim populations. If the most nationalistic among these forces would dare to brave the uncertainties of independence, the reason partly lies in the prospect of a pan-Islamic economic and political union, an idea whose chief advocate at the moment is Iran. In the Iranian version, such a union's nucleus would be an economic confederation of Caspian states, save for one—Russia—which goes unmentioned in Teheran's exhortations.

Uzbekistan, Turkmenistan, Tajikistan, Kyrgyzstan, and Azerbaijan have joined the Economic Cooperation Organization, recently formed by Iran, Turkey, and Pakistan. In February 1992 at a summit in Teheran, the group agreed to introduce preferential tariffs among members, found a development bank, and cooperate in modernizing transport, communications, industry, and agriculture. Russia, in turn, prefers the Black Sea grouping promoted by Turkish President Turgut Ozal. Indeed, all around the periphery of the former Soviet Union, states are banding together in regional economic clusters. The same month as the Central Asian states joined the Economic Cooperation Organization, Czechoslovakia, Hungary, Poland, and Ukraine were forming the Subcarpathian Council on Interregional Cooperation. Intended to facilitate trade among these states, the agreement establishes an interregional bank, free-trade zones, and special arrangements between state and private companies.

Thus the third major effect of the Soviet Union's collapse is the fracturing of structure where the international order meets what once was the impervious borders of the Soviet state. The result is an intense and complex regionalization of politics all around the Soviet periphery. This last feature, when combined with the two factors already discussed—the inchoate foreign policies of the successor states and the inherent prospects of instability within what used to be the USSR—should lead Western policy makers to suspect that the surprises and challenges of the post-Soviet period have scarcely begun.

But what is the range of possibilities? How grim or dramatic could these challenges become? And, how does one—how do Western policy makers—cope with an indeterminate environment whose spectrum of possibilities stretches afar?

First, the place to end is the place where I began: almost surely the degree of drama ahead will depend on what happens within these societies and, overwhelmingly, within Russia. If the progression toward stable, democratic political systems stops or spins off in another direction, the sources of deeper disorder—nationalistic passion, the temptation to meddle crudely or violently in the affairs of others, repression against one's own people, the aggrandizing of the military instrument, and the will to intimidate or crush opposition at home or next door—will be less easily contained. There is, of course, no guarantee that even further progress toward democracy will avoid all tendencies toward nationalistic provocations and heavy-handed diplomacy, but its opposite ensures that the pressures in this direction will grow immensely.

In this respect, two features of the present political environment are notable. First, despite their different stages of political development, as described in chapter 1, and despite their contrasting economic strategies, as described in chapter 2, in the most fundamental sense all of the new states are committed to the development of democratic political systems and market based economies. To a degree, these elementally common aspirations are a harness keeping the post-Soviet states within the same general forms of behavior and heightening the willingness and ability of national leaders to forgive or discount the excesses in a neighbor's actions (only to a point, however, as the war-torn relationship between Armenia and Azerbaijan proves).

Should this parallel circumstance give way to sharp differentials in development—that is, should the construction of democratic orders fall to a renewed authoritarianism in some states but not in others or should national leaderships adopt directly conflicting economic strategies—the natural sources of tension may not be easily deflected. If the contrasts emerge between Russia and Ukraine, the echo of tensions not easily deflected will be loud and far-reaching.

Because these are societies on the road to democracy, the impact on the matter of war and peace is not quite the often noted one of states already there. Common wisdom has it that democracies do not wage war against one another, for the sensible reason that they have nothing to gain by doing so.[16] If war be waged to make another country over in one's own image, the job is already done. If it be to achieve economic benefits, these are greater through normal economic intercourse. If it be to aggrandize the nation, more can be accomplished by other means. And if it be to enhance national security, liberal democratic partners are not the problem. Still, a linkage exists between the two cases. First, the effects of liberal democracy are present even in relations among states aspiring to democracy, albeit in far weaker and potentially ineffectual forms. Second, and more important, the moment a state gives up on its democratic strivings, the chance of one day achieving the full benefits to peace of relations between liberal democratic societies dies.

Second, although the dominant trend remains disintegration, there are within the political and economic environment, nationally and internationally, many countervailing trends. Thus while the old political and economic *systems* have yet to be replaced by new ones, many old political and economic *institutions* have been, and these provide an obstacle, albeit somewhat flimsy, against backsliding. Similarly, while the edge to nationalistic sensitivities is growing, the dampening effect of economic interdependence is not shrinking as fast. While the restlessness of Tatars, Buryats, and others within Russia mounts, the perils, both political and economic, of actually breaking with Moscow have scarcely disappeared. And so on.

Again, however, the effect will be very different if this "mixed" environment yields to one in which the forces of decay and violence begin to gallop, to reinforce one another, and to overwhelm all countervailing pressures. This would be an environment in which economic crisis, ethnic frictions, and political instability prevail singly and then together. (Within this trio, the decisive source of trouble—the one most capable of accelerating the other two— would appear to be an ever-deepening economic crisis.) Here too, the ultimate significance of the shift from one environment to another depends on where it occurs and among how many of the new states. If in Russia alone or Ukraine alone or in the two together, the consequences will be great. If across all of Central Asia, they are not likely to be enormously less great. Only if the shift occurs in or between one or two of the small states can we expect the consequences to remain confined.

If these are sound judgments, then Western policy makers should take heed. One crucial threshold marking the entry into a qualitatively different phase of trouble will be either the point at which any of the larger republics veers from the democratic path or the moment when the three crisis areas—economics, politics, and ethnicity—form a single juggernaut in any of the same republics. The two moments will doubtless have something to do with one another. Thus Western statesmen who warn of the perils of a failure of democratic transformation in Russia or Ukraine or across Central Asia and similarly of a deepening crisis within any of the three are right. The argument is not at all an example of poetic license.

Beneath the surface, obscured by the similarities in political and economic circumstance and muffled by the countervailing character of much of the change underway, rests a large issue whose future course will determine what is to become of this region and, consequently, what headaches it will generate for the world at large. The issue is Russia. Russia, both in fact and in the minds of its leaders, stands apart. It is the only potential great power among the successor states. While its liberal leaders of today are willing to acknowledge the reality and, more importantly, the legitimacy of independence for parts of the former empire, even they retain domineering habits of thought. For them, only Russia is a great power, and their new neighbors, while worthy of cooperation and respect, are simply not seen as states of the same consequence. Even when they accept the scaling back of their power and, with conviction, abjure the role of the predecessor state, they cannot think of themselves as anything other than the essence of what has been for 300 years. It is in everything, from the pride with which Yeltsin moved into Gorbachev's spacious Kremlin offices to the ease with which the General Staff imagines itself in command of Russia's armies.

This then creates a defining structural feature of the post-Soviet setting: within this new subsystem, one (potential) Great Power exists with a great many lesser, even inconsequential, powers. Moreover, this Great Power is not only the heir to an imperial past, whose scattered residue endures in many forms from the location of Russians abroad to the emotions of Russians at home, it is also a state aborning, struggling not merely to create a new order but to avoid dissolution. When Roman Szporluk in chapter

3 evokes the historic "German question," he is introducing a parallel worth pondering.

Academic international affairs specialists would see in this situation a fair test of their most basic notions about the game of nations. Some who believe that such a distribution of power guarantees a natural tendency toward tension and a good deal of wary, often friction-producing balancing actions by Russia's neighbors offer the rest of us fair warning. Others who believe that prevailing international norms, patterns of interdependence, and types of government (again, the matter of democracy) can short-circuit these effects offer us an alternative, but it is not one that happens of its own accord. Choices made within these societies will decide whether any or all of these influences grow stronger or weaker, and policies pursued by influential actors on the outside will in turn shape these choices. This is where Western policy comes in.

The natural tendency when trying to make one's way through fast-changing times is to focus on immediate, manifest dangers. By this standard, governments—both within the region and on the outside—tend to feature the daily parade of concerns: coping with violent ethnic conflicts in Nagorno-Karabakh and Moldova, responding to potential hunger in the Russian cities, buttressing the Gaidar reforms in Russia and encouraging equally radical steps in Ukraine, averting nuclear proliferation among the former Soviet republics and from them to other states, blocking Iranian inroads into Central Asia and Azerbaijan, and removing impediments like the Northern Territories issue in Russo-Japanese relations. This is not a mistaken agenda; on the contrary it is an utterly necessary one.

By the same standard, Western governments quickly decide what problems they cannot solve. They cannot ensure a democratic transformation within any of these states and even less their successful transition to vibrant market based economies. Nearly everyone agrees, not even together do the major states of the West have the economic wherewithal or the political leverage to bring about either outcome. At best they can make it easier for leaderships in these states to do the right thing, provided they are willing to do the right thing, for on that rests the destiny of change in these societies. Again, these are perfectly sound premises on which to base Western policy.

Yet while these are sensible ways to think about the problem, they miss its essence, and divorce policy from deeper historical stakes. What was once the Soviet Union is now an international arena, and in that arena the dynamic between Russia and its neighbors, one way or another, will determine which kind of politics is to prevail. In the end, it is in the interest of all of us on the outside that this arena—this subsystem of the larger order—acquire an underlying stability. In this sense, it is not merely the frictions of the moment between Russia and Ukraine that matter, but longer term trends in alignments, defense postures, and international institutions.

If what is today an unformed environment begins to evolve into one dominated by competitive alignments, offensive defense postures, and an absence of constraining institutions, global order will not be well served.

Today, when Lithuanian President Vitautas Landsbergis exhorts a confederation of the Baltic states, Belarus, and Ukraine, it is all a pipe dream, but, as one intelligent Russian observer has noted, the mere idea has an implicit "anti-Russian content," and, were it a reality, the military balance in this region would tilt against Russia.[17] Similarly, if Russia takes no special steps to reassure neighbors as it fashions a Russian military from the vast residue of the Red Army, or, if like its Soviet predecessor, it insists on the right to have military power equal to the combined resources of its new neighbors, others will answer in kind, and a degenerative process will have been set in motion. Similarly, if Russia's neighbors insist on destroying every last thread of security cooperation with it, and finding safety on their own, the Russian question is not likely to become easier.

On the other hand, if these states from the outset work to create a regime in which the security concerns of others are taken into account, the weak, protected, and the advantage goes to the defense, or more simply, if they seek mutual over unilateral security; if they assemble machinery for managing crises at least among lesser powers within their locale; if they strive for inclusive rather than exclusive groupings; and if they persist in a dialogue on these subjects, they will be marking out a very different road into the future. The West has no stake in urging Ukraine, Russia, and the others to preserve interrepublican institutions that prolong dysfunctional forms of cooperation, particularly, as Ericson notes in chapter 2, in the economic sphere. But it should want to see as much economic and security integration among these states as possible. It certainly should want the process of reconciling the national military postures of these states to begin immediately, while these postures are still in a formative stage. And it should want to encourage the development of effective crisis management mechanisms among these states.

For these things to happen, the West must act. First, the United States and other major powers should consciously and energetically use international institutions—the UN, the Conference on Security and Cooperation in Europe, the International Monetary Fund, and the World Bank—to foster these trends. International institutions embody norms that can and should be propagated within the region; they also can be used to reinforce complementary institutions created within the region. Second, in the next phase of arms control the West should take the lead in building a new post–Warsaw Pact security regime for Europe, not only including the new states of the former USSR, but pushing them to transform their own vicinity into an appropriate piece of the larger regime. Third, earlier rather than later is the time for Western powers to take an interest in the disputes between states like Russia and Ukraine, not hesitating to take positions on the merits of the issues involved and, in making their case, to invoke the standards of a world these states so much want to join.

In short, it would be historically short-sighted to conceive the post-Soviet challenge as only a matter of coping with a concrete range of instabilities, conflicts, and ruptured reforms, formidable as these may be. Instead, a new order—both within these post-Soviet societies and among them—is taking form, which over the next ten or fifteen years will harden into reality. Now, while the chance exists, the West has a powerful reason to want to help shape this order on *both* levels, not the least, because the two levels will surely interact.

It has been a central theme of these pages that, if the process goes wildly astray within the states themselves, nothing can save us or them from the consequences. But a wisely and carefully engineered international environment may help to see that this does not happen, and, along the way, can make a fundamental difference to the way troubled change is handled. Thus U.S. and Western policies should be consciously designed to influence developments on both levels, not merely those shaping the process of domestic reform. Returning to an earlier theme, if the liberal vision of international politics—one in which norms, elements of interdependence, and domestic structure matter—is to have a chance in this part of the world, it will require a good deal of Western intervention. Ahead, the future of the post-Soviet challenge and, at its core, the Russian question are likely to test more than academic theory and more than the peoples of the region.

Notes

[1] For the most part, Andrei Kozyrev has seemed to belong to this second group, but perhaps politics or Russian independence or long experience in the Soviet Union's Foreign Ministry are pushing him toward the first group.

[2] He made the comment in *The Diary of a Writer*. His purpose was to argue for a special Russian vocation in Asia, since in Europe Russia was a nation of "hangers-on and slaves," but the claim only underscored the conflicting pulls.

[3] Even Alexander Solzhenitsyn, who represents a neo-Slavophile version of this view, wants to bring a Western democratic tradition to Russia, and cares little about other areas bordering Russia, including Asia. (See, for example, his latest book, Solzhenitsyn [1991]).

[4] See his interview with V. Nadein in *Izvestiya,* December 26, 1991, p. 2.

[5] In a different but pertinent vein, said an unidentified senior Russian diplomat at the time of the first CIS meeting in Minsk in December, "In terms of its territory, Ukraine is another France, and in terms of its ambitions it's another China." (Mikhail Mayorov reporting on "Diplomatic Panorama," INTERFAX, January 3, 1992.)

[6] In *Uryadovyy Kuryer*, No. 38–39 (December 1991), p. 2, as reported in FBIS-SOV-92-006, January 9, 1992, pp. 61–62.

[7] See Yeltsin's address to the Russian Supreme Soviet as broadcast live on the Russian Television Network, February 13, 1992.

[8] This is in his major foreign policy statement in *Izvestiya,* January 2, 1992, p. 3.

[9] It does not sail by everyone. Tomas Kolesnichenko, an experienced Soviet international affairs correspondent, directly objected to these ideas as a warped "political orientation" that places too many hopes on the West and devalues necessary and important opportunities elsewhere in the world. (See his front-page article in *Pravda,* February 15, 1992, pp. 1 and 5.)

[10] *Pravda,* September 20, 1991, p. 2.

[11] See his lively interview with N. Zhelnorova in *Argumenty i fakty*, No. 8 (February 1992), pp. 1, 3–4.

[12] Vladimir Razuvayev, *Nezavisimaya gazeta,* March 5, 1992, p. 4.

[13] My own thinking on this and a number of related points has been much

influenced by a paper of his that is still in draft form, and entitled "The Future Strategic Relations between Former Soviet Republics."

¹⁴ Some of the details in this paragraph are drawn from Martha Brill Olcott, "Central Asia or Bust," *New York Times*, December 30, 1991, p. 15.

¹⁵ See, for example, Aleksei Chichkin's commentary on Radio Mayak, February 23, 1992, reported in FBIS-SOV-92-042, March 3, 1992.

¹⁶ Michael W. Doyle makes the argument best. See, for example, Doyle (1992).

¹⁷ Andrei Kortunov, in the draft of his paper, "The Future Strategic Relations between Former Soviet Republics."

6

Conclusion

TIMOTHY J. COLTON
AND ROBERT LEGVOLD

Not often does history topple empires, dispatch political systems, destroy an economic model, and cast aside a powerful idea-movement all at once, and never before without war. That all of this has happened without rupturing the world's peace or even without great violence and bloodshed within these societies is nearly miraculous. History's great convulsion, however, has not ended; it is but half-over. Having declared their independence, these fifteen former pieces of the Soviet Union must make of themselves states, and to do that they must form nations, while creating new political systems and new economic orders. Moreover, they must do so with the ruins of the old order everywhere weighing on their efforts. In particular, they must set about all this burdened by a deep economic crisis generated in the *ancien régime's* last years and then transferred to them.

If for this reason, the authors of this small book have been timid in predicting the outcome, the reader should not be surprised. Almost certainly it will be many years before the successor systems in the successor states have taken full and durable form. Along the way, as the preceding chapters make plain, conflicting trends and the fragility of new institutions are likely to produce various twists

and turns in the political development of this region. The likelihood that some of these societies may fall off the pace and back
into authoritarianism is great, and, even greater, the probability
that most of them, including Ukraine and Russia, will struggle at
the edge of economic crisis and political instability for years to
come.

History, like many other processes, is highly contingent: events
and choices at any given stage open and close the range of possible
events and choice at the next and subsequent stages. History, thus,
flows, not like a river, but like the branching of a tree. At moments,
when established forms, on which the next stage will be built, have
mostly collapsed, as in the former Soviet Union, the best one can
do is to understand the implications of current events and choices
for the next stage or two. When historical stages come in quick
succession, with the normal effect of decades, even centuries, com-
pressed into six-month periods—for example, the collapse of Soviet power in Eastern Europe in fall 1989, undoing forty-five years
of postwar history, the collapse of the Leninist system in the Soviet
Union in August 1991, undoing seventy-four years of twentieth-
century history, and the collapse of the Russian imperial state in
December 1991, undoing three or four centuries of modern European history—a lot of ground is covered in a hurry. If one pauses
for a moment to consider the stages through which Soviet history
has passed since Gorbachev came to power, and how far we are
from the starting point, and then imagines how many and far-
reaching the stages may be in the next decade or so, one soon loses
the urge to predict the shape of things five years from now, let
alone ten or fifteen.

The authors of this book certainly have no such urge. They
have taken as their task to identify what is seminal in the events of
the current stage and to highlight the choices that will make a
difference, not for ten years from now, but in the next stage or two.
In doing so they have, quite independently of one another, con-
structed a study comprising related and, to a striking degree, common themes.

Integrating the Pieces

Several important threads run through this book. Disorder is one, but the disorder has two sides, one creative, the other destructive. The interlinked character of the challenges facing these new states is another. The powerful effect of the Soviet legacy is a third. And the importance of choice and leadership is a fourth.

Creative Disorder

All five authors, in one fashion or another, stress the cumulative effect of the disintegration of Soviet institutions, practices, and mentalities. This falling apart has brought forth a disorder so profound and so pervasive as to penetrate every major facet of early post-Soviet affairs.

In politics, Colton notes, we have witnessed both a shattering of the long-established form of government and a drastic reduction in the degree of effective governance. Richard Ericson compares what is left of the planned economy to a corpse that has been decapitated but whose parts manage here and there to perform some of their prior functions. The extinction of a Soviet identity once uniting these peoples is the point of departure for Roman Szporluk's chapter. Stephen Meyer traces the disarray in the military and defense industrial establishments, both of them beset by the loss of shared purpose, prestige, funding, and political support. And post-Soviet foreign policy, in Legvold's reading, has collapsed into conceptual chaos, the more or less helpless creature of internal preoccupations.

How should we be evaluating these remarkable changes? In the first instance, as nearly all the authors argue, the changes have been benign and necessary. The disintegration of the Soviet Union has in part been a manifestation of creative disorder.

In the political sphere, anti-Communist forces have pushed to near completion the job of destroying the authoritarian Soviet system begun by the last leader of the Communist party, Mikhail Gorbachev. De-Sovietization has left all fifteen republics in at least a predemocratic stage and committed, in one degree or another, to building democracy. In the economy, the tide of change has disabled allocative mechanisms based by and large on doctrinal and political imperatives, rather than on the logic of efficiency. Burgeoning uncertainty has forced state firms to seek out fresh sources of supply and has given nonstate enterprise some room to grow. The emancipation of the republics has put an end to Europe's only remaining colonial empire. To the non-Russians and the Russians themselves, de-Sovietization offers the opportunity of normal modernization under conditions of national independence, not dissimilar to those enjoyed by comparable groups in most other areas of the globe.

We can take equal reassurance from watershed events in the realms of national security and foreign policy. The crippling of the armed forces and of the vast infrastructure that underpinned their growth removes the traditional Soviet military threat. It also hands post-Soviet politicians a sterling chance to reassign scarce resources to long-neglected investment and welfare needs. In world politics, the anxious, revisionist state that was a destabilizing force since the Bolshevik Revolution no longer exists. There seems little likelihood that a geographically, economically, and militarily diminished Russia will fill the vacated Soviet role. No one need weep over its passing or over the disappearance of the internally repressive aspects of Soviet rule.

Dangers

The same developments, however, have another negative side, which neither the ex-Soviets nor we on the outside dare ignore. For one thing, the disorder of the last half-decade, fertile as it has been in certain respects, has not yet been nearly enough by itself to permanently solve the enormous problems that generated the crisis of the Soviet regime. Altered and in most instances gravely exacerbated by incomplete and unsuccessful reforms, these problems have now been thrown in the laps of the successor states.

In government, the dictate of Moscow and the guidance of the Communist party apparatus are gone, but democratic legislatures, cohesive executive organs, and capable bureaucracies are at best half-formed. So too are the political parties and other private organizations required to join state institutions to society. The eco-

nomic crisis in the republics deepens with every month's production statistics, with the odds being that things will get a good deal
worse before they begin to get better. The collapse of the Soviet
state, while satisfying the aspirations of previously subordinated
minorities, has opened up a "Russian problem" that Szporluk
reminds us has many of the features of the classic "German problem" in European politics, a problem that produced two world
wars in this century. The frailty of the Commonwealth of Independent States (CIS) and the resolve of several of the republics to build
their own armed forces have left much of the former Soviet military command and defense production establishment in a bizarre
stateless condition, caught between competing allegiances and
helpless to prevent the withering of their assets. By the same token,
de-Sovietization has given rise to a fragile and tense international
milieu where before there had been a stable, unified national entity in which one central power in Moscow dampened conflicts at
the periphery.

Moreover, the pressures toward further fragmentation and
deterioration in the former Soviet space have not yet crested. Ericson, in his chapter, comments on the adoption of beggar-thy-
neighbor trade policies and the "feudalization" of the post-Soviet
economy behind regional walls. Along similar lines, Meyer sees
the eruption of "degenerate conversion," uncoordinated and
wasteful of resources and technology, within the once paramount
armaments industry. Colton describes a "regionalization" of government and politics and a tendency for disorder and uncertainty
still growing, which threatens the construction of needed new institutions. And Szporluk warns that centrifugal forces grounded in
ethnicity are gaining in strength in several of the independent
republics. As they interact with interrepublic rivalries, they
heighten the chances of violence dwarfing in scale and intensity
the battles over Nagorno-Karabakh.

In the Soviet order, the leadership used national security imperatives to justify the maintenance of domestic controls. After the
Soviet Union, however, foreign policy and military factors are in
some ways reinforcing the disintegration of state structures. The
international relations of the new states tug them and their sundry
parts in different directions. Central Asia is wooed by Iran and

Turkey, the Far East explores cooperation with Japan and the Baltic countries with Scandinavia, and Moldova discusses unification with Rumania. Against these pressures, the CIS and what remains of the Soviet economic planning apparatus are feeble counterweights. Meyer depicts the army officer corps as demoralized and adrift, and both he and Ericson write of the localization of decision authority within the military-industrial complex. From here it would be but one short step for professional soldiers to transfer their loyalties to subrepublic governments, perhaps breeding a post-Soviet form of the regional warlordism that plagued China before 1949.

Linkages among Problems

No theme emerges more clearly from the preceding chapters than the linked character of the problems and crises facing the new states. Our authors agree that these connections are rich, varied, and synergetic, with a potential for causing great disruption in future.

Economic problems, for example, powerfully accentuate the political and ethnic difficulties of the successor states. Queuing, declines in production, and macroeconomic imbalances sap governmental authority and enlarge budget deficits. Retail price increases and the early warning signs of factory closings and mass unemployment stir resistance to the new, market-minded elites. The lack of clarity about property ownership blurs boundaries between public and private spheres, encouraging corruption and the abuse of office. Just as the economic shortcomings of communism discouraged formation of a common Soviet identity, the failure of Gorbachev's efforts to reform the Soviet economy stimulated the emergence of nationalist challenges to Moscow's rule in key republics.

Conversely, political and ethnic realities burden economic solutions. Constitutional confusion and administrative incapacity limit the ability of governments to devise and implement radical economic reforms. Ironically, the systems of budding democracy are also constraining economic reformers, as social groups disadvantaged by marketizing change, and elites sympathetic with those groups, are taking advantage of the new openness of the political system to protest and obstruct policies that are probably meritorious from a narrowly economic point of view. Relations between ethnic communities have become sufficiently inflamed in some republics—Azerbaijan and Moldova are the limiting cases—as to submerge economic reform issues. And ethnicity and political institutions, needless to say, are themselves interlocked in a multiplicity of ways in all the post-Soviet republics.

Nearly all of our authors have also emphasized the special significance and complexity of the interactions between the external and internal contexts of the republics' affairs. Thus, for example, the end of the cold war and the world trend toward democracy probably enhance the prospects of democratic consolidation in Russia, Ukraine, and the other politically advanced republics. If the fracturing of interrepublic trade based on the command principle has had a certain utility in terms of economic reform, furtherance of reform will require reknitting of the republics' economies on a more selective and a more rational foundation. Given the massive interdependence of the republics in the Soviet era, their internal decisions in the post-Soviet era are closely bound up with their relations with one another. One particular interrepublican relationship—that between Russia and Ukraine—dominates in importance all others. Although Russian-Ukrainian cooperation is no guarantee of success on the economic and political fronts, a breakdown in the relationship would handicap reform and reconstruction prospects in all areas. The worst imaginable outcome—a military confrontation between the two that would make the civil war in Yugoslavia look tame—would likely put the marketization and democratization processes on indefinite hold in the better part of the former Soviet Union.

The Importance of the Legacy

In thinking about the present and looking to the middle-term future, the analysis of this book lays heavy stress on the continued weight of the past. The Soviet legacy is especially influential, above all as a constraint on governments.

The political inheritance of seven decades of Communist party

rule includes a disrespect for constitutional norms, stunted governmental institutions, and a poorly ramified and underorganized
civil society. All three deficits are obstacles to democratic development. The economic inheritance contains several key impediments to marketization: an absence of enforceable property rights;
the lack of real money and of a capable taxation system; primitive
social safety nets; and a widespread popular hostility toward commercial activity. Ethnic relations in the 1990s and beyond will
continue to be affected by Stalin's arbitrary drawing of republic
boundaries, which placed large national minorities within each
union republic, and by the hierarchical ranking of republics and
lesser ethnic homelands. The question of all ethnic questions will
be about the Russians, whose dilemma is to decide whether they
are to be empire builders or to seek their destiny in a nation-state,
a choice never fully resolved under Soviet auspices. Foreign policy
makers in the republics, meanwhile, take over institutions—from
foreign ministries and spy agencies to diplomatic academies and
think tanks—designed from the outset to serve the needs of a
Russian directed military superpower, and difficult to adapt to the
goals of much smaller countries with very different ambitions.

There are legacies as well from *perestroika* and from the extreme
turmoil of 1989–92. Political reform in the late 1980s gave the
Soviet peoples competitive elections, legislatures with a mind of
their own, and an end to the Communists' dominance. In addition, it gave them legislative-executive infighting, fractious parliamentary parties with shallow roots in society, and reliance on
edicts of dubious legality to vanquish the Communist party. As an
economic legacy, the last years of Soviet rule bequeathed the post-
Soviet leaders a disaster so acute and so riddled with discrete problems that politicians are easily distracted from chronic and over-
arching questions. The military, for its part, inherits a vacuum of
state authority at the former USSR level and a melting industrial
base.

The Importance of Leadership and of Policy

The focus of this book has often been on systemic variables. Yet
the authors also implicitly and explicitly have put much stress on

the human factor. Without denying the importance of large-scale social, economic, and political forces and processes, we reserve a critical role for leadership and policy.

The *perestroika* that led to the demise of the Soviet regime would not have been undertaken in the sequence and ways it was without decisions taken by particular personalities. It was Gorbachev's genius to pinpoint the urgency of reforms; it was his failing to anticipate and contain the consequences of his own measures, thereby kindling a life-and-death crisis of the system that he set out to rescue. Boris Yeltsin, beginning as a lieutenant of Gorbachev, had the resolve and the sense of the possibilities imminent in the situation to break with Gorbachev in 1987, to press him from the left once electoral reform was instituted in 1989, and to squeeze Gorbachev and the central state out of the picture after August 1991. Had their roles been reversed, it is entirely possible that the outcome would have been different, or at the very least that it would have been delayed.

Post-Soviet politics already offers clear instances of both creative and failed leadership making a difference. In Ukraine, Leonid Kravchuk has deftly balanced competing interests, outmaneuvered opponents, and reassured social groups, such as the large Russian minority in the republic, who might otherwise have fought Ukraine's movement to independence. In Georgia, on the other hand, Zviad Gamsakhurdia squandered an overwhelming popular mandate, proving incapable either of restraining himself and his followers or of neutralizing his adversaries. Only one month after Kravchuk won direct election as president and secured the consent of all major components of the population to his line on sovereignty in a referendum, Gamsakhurdia was ousted in an ugly and violent coup d'état.

If statesmanship and political perspicacity can make a difference, so too can enlightened and well-crafted policies. This is especially important to keep in mind when one thinks of the staggering contextual problems that lie before all of the post-Soviet governments. Economic, ethnic, and other difficulties more or less force governments to respond; they do not force them to respond wisely. Nor do contexts evolve independently of what governments and elites do. Policy, as has been argued in this book, can decisively shape context, changing the political environment for better or for worse.

Radical economic reform, for example, was stymied under Gorbachev, in no small measure because his government never articulated coherent programs that would push it forward. Economic transformation will now move ahead only to the extent that post-Soviet governments invent laws, institutional mechanisms, and other protections that will foster genuine nonstate ownership and market coordination. Real property, real money, and real markets will not drop ready-made from the sky. They have to be encouraged, as Ericson writes, by real and farsighted policies. Reformist policies must be tempered by political realities, as we already observe in Russia, and as would be the case in any society, but political realism is not the same as lack of vision and will.

The same applies to the management of ethnic relations in what are all multiethnic societies. Szporluk notes the conciliatory approach toward national minorities in Ukraine, where the Kravchuk government and most Ukrainian nationalists embrace a political and geographic definition of citizenship. Because Russians and other ethnic non-Ukrainians do not feel excluded, they have gone along with the ethnic majority and there has been relatively little strain between communities. In some other republics of the former Soviet Union, by contrast, citizenship has been defined in less tolerant ethnic and linguistic terms, with the result that conflict has increased and some minority leaders have become implacable opponents of the present governments.

Foreign relations is yet another field where the quality of policy can make and has made a difference. Tensions among the successor states are natural and unavoidable, yet need not be unmanageable. Extreme claims and the willingness of Azerbaijan and Armenia to see conflict escalate have produced the nightmare of Nagorno-Karabakh. Between Russia and Ukraine, however, common sense and moderation have thus far kept the two republics' disputes from boiling over into violence, despite episodes that might easily have done so. One can only hope that it is the Russia-Ukraine model of interrepublic relations, not the Azerbaijan-Armenia model, that prevails in future.

Challenge and Choice: The West
and the Post-Soviet Reality

Although this book is mainly about the evolution of post-Soviet developments, we would not want to end the analysis without offering some thoughts on the challenge posed for the outside world by the continuing drama—thoughts that are our own, and not necessarily those of our fellow authors. We do not pretend to know what Western governments should do about this or that specific problem. But we do have a sense of the larger context, and perhaps more usefully, a notion of how the larger pieces might be put together.

Most people, we suspect, sense that this is one of those special historical moments, the kind that only come once in a century, when time seems to speed up and history catapults forward. Each of the last two centuries concluded with accelerated, turbulent, tragically fecund decades that defined the century to follow, but only after awful denouements. Again we are experiencing the intensity of an "end of century." Whether ahead lie tragedies on a scale matching earlier ages we cannot any more foretell than our counterparts could in 1792 or 1892. Until the evidence mounts, we would rather draw our insights from another cycle.

Twice before in this century the United States and its allies faced the challenge of postwar reconstruction—unsuccessfully after the First World War, successfully after the Second World War—and this might be thought of as a third occasion. Before us stands the challenge of post–cold war reconstruction. In large part we, principally North America, Western Europe, and Japan, succeeded the second time because we learned the lessons of our failure the first time. Assuming that we are still wiser, because to the lessons of failure we now add the lessons of success, there should be no reason to worry. But this further assumes that the stakes are understood to be as great today as they were forty-five years ago, and that we are as able to act as our predecessors.

How should we think about the stakes? Secretary of State James Baker has used the metaphor of mountain climbers tethered by the same rope, implying that if the Russians lose their hold, we will all be flung into the abyss. Richard Nixon has said that if democracy fails in Russia it will bring a new despotism whose imperial nature could be "far more threatening to the world than the old communism." For most people, however, apocalyptic judgments of this sort are not persuasive. People may not have trouble imagining a good deal of misery, instability, and conflict in Russia and her neighbors, but they do not see how this is likely to affect the safety and welfare of the United States. Even the failure of the democratic experiment in Russia, sad as that would be, does not for them translate into self-evident dangers to American interests.

Much of the problem stems from the gap between our historic stakes, which could, indeed, be immense, and our immediate stakes, which appear to be far more modest. The heirs of what used to be the world's largest state, a space constituting one-sixth of the earth's surface, are making fundamental choices, are setting a fateful course. If, in the end, they become a part of the West, not merely aspiring to our institutions and values, but successfully adopting them, the world will be one kind of place. If they fail, and take another path, or if the ongoing struggle consigns them to the lot of much of the south, it will be another kind of place.

Perhaps it helps to remind ourselves that this region is not simply an out-of-the-way part of the globe. It is Eurasia's heartland. Physically it links Asia, including an economically dynamic East Asia, to Europe, historically the United States' ultimate international priority. If this heartland, an area of enormous natural wealth with skilled and talented peoples, can reach the point of economic take-off over the next ten to fifteen years, the well-being of Europe, Asia, and others, including the United States, in the twenty-first century will be considerably, maybe even immeasurably, enhanced.

Conversely, if this region sinks into economic degradation and extended crisis, Asia and Europe will not escape the consequences, and if they do not, neither will the United States. The problem is magnified by an important peculiarity: all around the outer rim of the former Soviet Union, from North Korea to Poland, in unrelenting succession, exist states whose own economic and political futures are in doubt. Rather than a buffer against the effects of misfortune in the former Soviet Union, they are more likely to act as a transmission belt into the wider world.

Misfortune, in this case, may take many different forms, and rather than try to describe them all, it seems more helpful to offer several illustrations of the trouble that may lie ahead. First, and gravest, would be war between Russia and Ukraine—a highly improbable event as things now stand, but given trends, no longer utterly unthinkable. Should it come to pass, it would be the first war among major European powers in half a century. Immediate neighbors, such as Poland, Hungary, and Czechoslovakia, run a serious risk of being drawn in, and Europe's major powers, too, would not find it as easy as in, say, Yugoslavia's recent wars to hold themselves above the conflict, playing the role of disinterested mediators. But even intense political conflict short of war, a less improbable prospect, would create strains far beyond the borders of these two countries.

Second, it hardly seems a flight of imagination to foresee one or more of these new countries, including the largest among them, suffering levels of internal instability and disarray on a scale too great to be kept within national borders. If the instability seems likely to aid elements viewed as inimical to the interests of outsiders, it will be difficult for outsiders to resist meddling. And even if outsiders control the temptation to interfere, they may not be able to shield themselves from the effects of turmoil: large numbers of desperate people in flight, the loss of control over large stocks of armaments, terrorism, and the accelerating export of ecological decay.

Third, and related to the last category, there are signs already that not merely one or two, but a swelling number of these post-Soviet states may be the nucleus of new regional conflicts from one end of the former Soviet Union to the other. The bloodiest and earliest of these conflicts, the confrontation between Armenia and Azerbaijan over Nagorno-Karabakh, has been largely confined to the warring parties, but the moment Russia began to distance itself from the conflict and commonwealth forces were withdrawn, other parties, including the Turks and the Iranians, moved in.

A potentially graver crisis came along in Moldova in March 1992, when Moldovan authorities decided to repress forcefully the renegade military forces of the breakaway Dniester republic, the eastern half of Moldova, dominated by 600,000 Slavs. Instantly

Russian, Ukrainian, and Rumanian interests were engaged: Russian interests, first, because most of the Slav inhabitants of the region are Russian; and second, because the former Soviet 14th Army remained in the area; Ukrainian interests, first, because one-third of the 600,000 were Ukrainians, thousands of whom immediately began streaming across the border as refugees; second, because Don Cossacks crossed Ukraine to join the fray; and third, because Moscow talked of using the 14th Army to impose a peace; and Rumanian interests, because Bucharest lays claim to the whole area.

Neither of these conflicts seems likely to fade into insignificance any time soon. Instead, still other points of regional instability along the frontiers of the ex-USSR may emerge, introducing pockets of international violence all along Eurasia's inner rim. Each of these, taken alone, may be no more damaging to the larger fabric of international relations than regional conflicts of the past, but taken together, they may have a cumulative effect that is far more original and dangerous. Tajikistan, Turkmenistan, and an increasingly turbulent Afghanistan well might constitute one such further nexus. Were nationalist forces in Xinjiang or Inner Mongolia to gather strength in the coming Chinese political succession, these territories, their suddenly unpredictable neighbors in Central Asia, and China could create another.

And fourth, even without great political turmoil or conflict, a deepening economic crisis within Russia or Ukraine promises considerable grief for the outside world. In the short run, economic paralysis adds to the specter of renewed tragedy among Russia and Ukraine's decrepit nuclear power plants, as governments are helpless to find the resources needed to close down most of the sixteen Chernobyl-type facilities. It also threatens to turn an $80 billion external debt into a definitive default, the principal impact of which will fall on European banks and governments. Then there are the effects of a still larger disruption in post-Soviet trade with fragile East European economies. And for the world's great petroleum-importing states, Russia will cease to be an incremental and alternative source. A complete economic collapse would not only magnify these and other economic effects, but almost surely stimulate either massive public unrest or an end to democracy or both.

In short, the potential stakes are large. But that only raises the second question: can the United States do anything about them? Can it ensure that the worst does not happen, or that the best does? The straightforward answer is not alone and, even with others, not decisively, by which we mean not as the architect of solutions, positive steps, intelligent choices that are not already pursued by the countries of the region. The commonplace that we cannot do for them what they will not do for themselves is correct. So is the corollary that the outside world's influence exists only at the margin.

While true enough, neither proposition contains much help for Western policy. In the last postwar reconstruction we also could not do for them (the Germans, French, British, Japanese, and others) what they would not do for themselves. But when they were ready "to do for themselves," we could and did make a vast difference. Similarly, exerting influence at the margin scarcely means no influence; the margin can be critical. Thus the real challenge is how to be effective at the margin.

Often the issue is reduced to helping the new states or not and on what scale—helping them materially by providing various forms of economic assistance or practically by sending an infinite variety of experts to teach them how to build new political, economic, and social institutions. This seems to us too narrow an approach. In this book the authors have been describing a ramified, many-tiered, intricately linked challenge. It should not be reduced to a single dimension. On the contrary, to be effective, U.S. and Western policy must recognize that the task is manifold, spread across many different spheres.

For example, there are in Russia, Ukraine, and Lithuania sixteen RBMK graphite-moderated reactors that Ivan Selin, the chair of the U.S. Nuclear Regulatory Commission, calls "an enormous hazard," which should be shut down as soon as possible, because they "share the same fundamentally unstable physics which are unique to the Chernobyl-type reactors. They have only a rudimentary safety system, plus they have a basic instability called positive reactivity" (the hotter the reaction gets the more efficient it becomes, and, therefore, still hotter).[1] Merely to retrofit the remaining and moderately safer non-RBMK reactors will exceed $7.5 billion, and, in the meantime, if safety is to be enhanced through the use of computers, better training, antifire measures (such as shielded cables, insulated hot-spots, replacement of tar roofs, and the like), and technically improved control rods, the help will have to come from the West.

Or to select another illustration still farther from the aid issue (as defined by the International Monetary Fund (IMF) and key Western governments): if the new states do not handle well the potent challenges of multiethnicity, if they choose the discriminatory, blood based interwar approach to nation building described by Szporluk, tensions will rise within these societies and relations between them will be inflamed. Neither the United States nor other major powers should treat this issue as beyond their power to influence.

These two very different sorts of problems only begin to sketch the diversity of the challenge. From health care (already the dangers of full-scale epidemics of polio, diphtheria, and whooping cough are too high because increasing numbers of children are going unvaccinated) to nuclear proliferation (Russia's three neighbors are not with speed and alacrity settling the issue), the tasks for U.S. policy are many and still growing.[2] As Legvold's earlier chapter suggests, they involve not only abetting the transformation within these societies, but the creation of a stable international environment among them. Promoting safer and less threatening military postures among these states is as important as facilitating modern banking systems within them. Involving the international community in dispute resolution between any two of them matters as much as improving the climate for foreign investment in any one of them.

Because, when it comes to the grand drama underway in the former Soviet Union, Western policies, including that of the United States, can influence trends only at the margin, two requirements are particularly important. First is American leadership of a larger Western effort. No country by itself has the means to make a difference; only all the industrial democracies taken together can do that; and for such to happen the United States must lead. Other countries, as Germany has already demonstrated, are capable of considerable initiative, but none can weld the policies of the Group of Seven nations into a more potent, better coordinated whole.

Leadership does not mean putting up the lion's share of economic assistance, but it does mean pulling one's weight. Trumpeting one's contribution to humanitarian aid for Russia, when it amounts to one-tenth of 1 percent of Germany's less trumpeted contribution, is not pulling one's weight. Neither is it, when Congress refuses to provide the United States' expected contribution to the IMF, permitting the fund to deal with a number of needs among which are a mutually agreed aid program to Russia, or when it refuses to pay UN peacekeeping dues. More positively, it means helping to design a more coherent and integrated set of Western responses to the full range of challenges generated by this region, the political as well as the economic ones.

The other requirement is for a comprehensive and integrated U.S. policy toward the region. Because so many of the problems raised by the former republics of the Soviet Union are interlinked, so must the response be. Ultimately the problems of nuclear proliferation within the former Soviet Union, of arms flows to the Third World from the region, of destabilizing military postures among the new states, and the fate of arms control agreements, such as START and the CFE treaty, are all connected. If they are addressed separately and in isolation, or, worse, some of them not at all, the odds of failure increase. Similarly if U.S. policy makers worry only about the transfer of Western institutions and techniques to these societies, and neglect to insist on a standard of human rights and peaceful change set by the international institutions into which all of these societies have eagerly enrolled, the effort to foster democracy will be correspondingly weaker. The list of illustrations is far longer than U.S. policy to this point or the national discussion of it suggests.

Finally, policy, it seems to us, would be well-served if it kept uppermost several simple guidelines, beyond the need for a collective and coherent response. First, given the magnitude of potential trouble in this region, avoiding crises should be a priority objective, rather than trying to cope with them after they are already a reality. Crisis prevention is a difficult task, requiring far more effective international machinery than is yet in place, but crisis management, where most of the postwar effort has been to date, does not stand much of a chance in this setting—not if things go really wrong.

Second, a successful policy toward this region will likely require a combination of patience and determination not always evident in postwar U.S. international involvements. Nothing can be done to resolve the fate of these new states in a year or two. The struggle will unfold over many years, and if the United States is to have a meaningful role to play, its commitment must be for years to come. Policy must be designed for the long-haul, not primarily for the moment. It also needs to be fortified against the disappointed expectations that will almost surely intervene at various times in the years ahead. Russia and her neighbors are not likely to march as steadily and reliably toward democracy, economic stability, and our way of life as many now hope.

Finally, never has it been more important to recognize our long-term stakes and to place them ahead of our short-term preferences. Sacrificing for the long run, instead of managing only the short run, and expending effort and money now in order to avoid expending a great deal more later are principles by which many of our people live their personal lives, but not ones they encourage their government to live by. Yet if this book has been about anything, it is that the future of these new states and, with them, of an important part of the twenty-first century, are being determined now.

Notes

[1] *Wel/My,* April 1992, pp. 1, 2.
[2] On the health issue and what to do about it, see Arthur Hartman, "Life or Death for Russian Children," *New York Times,* February 25, 1992, p. A21.

Bibliography

Allison, Graham, and Gregory F. Treverton. eds. 1992. *Rethinking America's Security*. New York: W.W. Norton.

Commission on Security and Cooperation in Europe. 1992. *The Referendum on Independence and Presidential Election in Uzbekistan, December 29, 1991*. Washington, D.C.: U.S. Commission on Security and Cooperation in Europe.

Di Palma, Giuseppe. 1990. *To Craft Democracies: An Essay on Democratic Transitions*. Berkeley and Los Angeles: University of California Press.

Doyle, Michael. 1992. "An International Liberal Community." In Allison and Treverton 1992.

Ericson, Richard E. 1991. "The Classical Soviet-Type Economy: Nature of the System and Implications for Reform." *Journal of Economic Perspectives*, Vol. 5, No. 4.

Huntington, Samuel P. 1968. *Political Order in Changing Societies*. New Haven and London: Yale University Press.

———. 1991. *The Third Wave: Democratization in the Late Twentieth Century*. Norman and London: University of Oklahoma Press.

Lewin, Moshe. 1989. *The Gorbachev Phenomenon. A Historical Interpretation*. Berkeley and Los Angeles: University of California Press.

Meyer, Stephen M. 1991/92. "How the Threat (and the Coup) Collapsed:

The Politicization of the Soviet Military." *International Security*, Vol. 16, No. 3 (Winter 1991/92).

O'Donnell, Guillermo, and Philippe C. Schmitter. 1986. *Transitions from Authoritarian Rule: Tentative Conclusions about Uncertain Democracies.* Baltimore and London: Johns Hopkins Press.

Pipes, Richard. 1968. *The Formation of the Soviet Union: Communism and Nationalism, 1917–1923.* New York: Atheneum.

Solzhenitsyn, Alexander. 1991. *Rebuilding Russia: Reflections and Tentative Proposals.* Translated by Alexis Klimoff. New York: Farrar, Straus and Giroux.

Szporluk, Roman. 1981. *The Political Thought of Thomas G. Masaryk.* Boulder, Co.: East European Monographs.

———. 1989. "Dilemmas of Russian Nationalism." *Problems of Communism* (July–August 1989).

Touraine, Alain. 1988. *Return of the Actor: Social Theory in Postindustrial Society.* Translated by Myrna Godzich. Minneapolis: University of Minnesota Press.

Williams, Colin. 1985. "Conceived in Bondage—Called unto Liberty: Reflections on Nationalism." *Progress in Human Geography*, Vol. 9, No. 3 (September 1985).

Williams, Colin, and Anthony D. Smith. 1983. "The National Construction of Social Space." *Progress in Human Geography*, Vol. 7, No. 4 (December 1983).

Yeltsin, Boris. 1990. *Against the Grain: An Autobiography.* Translated by Michael Glenny. New York: Summit Books.

Index